LITHUANIAN
CHRISTIAN
DEMOCRACY

"The Baltic States should be
sovereign independent peoples..."
Winston Churchill

Emblem design by A. Kulpa

The several elements of the Lithuanian Christian Democratic emblem depicted on the cover are symbolic of Christianity, Lithuanianism and Democracy. The three main principles are symbolized by the three crosses, which at the same time remind Lithuanians of the Mount of Three Crosses in the ancient capital of Lithuania - Vilnius. The crosses long since have been torn down by the Soviet occupiers. The outline of the globe symbolizes Christian Democracy's reach throughout the world. The symbol at the base of the crosses, called the Gediminas Columns, represents a gate in a fortified wall or a castle. It is believed that it symbolized the sovereignty of Grand Duke Gediminas. Later, together with the Knight, it was used by Lithuanian rulers as a national emblem. "LKDS" at the base is an acronym for Lietuvių Krikščionių Demokratų Sąjunga, the Lithuanian language name of the Lithuanian Christian Democratic Union.

LITHUANIAN CHRISTIAN DEMOCRACY

by ALGIRDAS J. KASULAITIS

Library of Congress Catalog Card Number: 75-43376

Published by Leo XIII Fund
Affiliate of the Lithuanian Christian Democratic Union

First Edition, 1976

Printed in the United States of America
by
"Draugas"
4545 West 63rd Street
Chicago, Ill. 60629

CONTENTS

FOREWORD

I

In most instances, it is a joy to witness the publication of another book on Christian Democracy. *Lithuanian Christian Democracy* by Algirdas J. Kasulaitis is certainly one.

By their accomplishment, the author, and the Lithuanian Christian Democratic Union of which he is a former Chairman, have served the cause and study of both Christian Democracy and Lithuanian nationhood.

Many books and articles are published on Christian Democracy, but the majority of them are in languages other than English. The Christian Democratic Center and the Christian Democratic Movement exist to promote, respectively, the study and practice of Christian Democracy in English speaking nations. Thus, we are gratified that *Lithuanian Christian Democracy* has been published in English.

Not all books on Christian Democracy necessarily edify it; especially ones which must truthfully report on incomplete or partially erroneous ideologies and programs, schisms within the parties, and failures of leaders and organizations. Happily, this is not the case with *Lithuanian Christian Democracy*. From the elaboration and publication of the Lithuanian Christian Democratic program in 1904-1907, to the Party's leadership in the 1920-22 Constituent Assembly, to the Party's governance of Lithuania from 1922 to 1926, and to the present struggle of Lithuanian national liberation, Lithuanian Christian Democrats have shown a purity of ideology and performance equal to any Christian Democratic movement or party in the world.

The sad part of the book is that it must recount a history of suffering by the Lithuanian people and nation, also equal to that experienced by any other cultural, national, racial, or religious group in the world. "Liberation" is a watchword of many new nations today; of national groups seeking a return to their homelands, such as Palestinians; and of large minority groups within nations seeking treatment equal to that of the majority population, such as Blacks in the United States. Lithuanians are struggling for all three forms of Liberation. Through military might, the Soviet Union invaded Lithuania on June 15, 1940, and has cruelly oppressed the Lithuanian people ever since. Thus, Lithuanians, and other believers in democracy, must liberate the Lithuanian nation itself, liberate it so that Lithuanians throughout the world may return home, and guarantee human rights to Lithuanians who are living within the Soviet Union and other East European communist countries.

One of the lessons we are learning only now in the United States is that it is unrealistic to promote political democracy unless we also work for economic democracy at the same time. Lithuanian Christian Democrats were farsighted in understanding this. The 1904 Program (see Chapter 7), adopted by an organizational meeting of Christian Democrats in 1907, called for a democracy for "poor people" in its preamble, and outlined specific economic programs in its fifth chapter. Among these were distribution of land to peasants, organization of credit unions, and public welfare programs, hospitals, nursing homes, sick benefits, and social security — all for the poor. As Algirdas Kasulaitis rightly emphasizes, referring to these economic programs and the whole Christian Democratic Program of 1904, "it must be borne in mind that these theses were expounded... at a time when democracy in Europe, as we understand it today, was in its infancy."

The most powerful statement in the 1904 Program is found in its preamble. It reads, "We call ourselves Christians and use this word in our organization title because we believe that there is a God and that Christ is our Redeemer. We accept the teachings of Jesus and His laws we shall obey." I agree. Jesus Christ is the foundation of Christian Democracy. Without Him there can be no movement or party, nor any democracy.

It is this explicit commitment to Jesus which, I believe, enabled Lithuanian Christian Democracy to avoid the dichotomy between capitalism and socialism-communism in which so many aspiring democracies have been trapped. Kasulaitis does not mention such a debate in his detailed account of the historical and internal development of Lithuanian Christian Democracy, so we can only assume that it was non-existent or not very important.

The dilemma of the dichotomy goes somewhat like this. Some democracies only establish political democracy and do not confront economic inequities. Eventually, uncontrolled greed, most often capitalism, leads to corruption or overthrow of the democracies from the right. Socialism-communism is then offered as an alternative. This solves nothing. Capitalism was a mistake. Socialism-communism is a mistaken response to a mistake. And two mistakes do not make a "right." The answer is to return to true and complete democracy — economic and political. I dwell on this point because, as you read Kasulaitis' study, it is very evident that the Lithuanian Christian Democrats came to grips with the challenge of economic democracy from the very foundation of their movement and of the modern era of their nation.

Beginning with the Constituent Assembly of 1920, the Christian Democrats moved forthrightly toward economic democracy. As Kasulaitis explains, Lithuania was primarily an agricultural economy. And in such an economy, where land is the primary means of production, the distribution of land to as many persons as possible is the method of establishing economic democracy. This is exactly what the Lithuanian Christian Democrats did. Under the leadership of Father Mykolas Krupavičius, as Minister of Agriculture in the new Lithuanian government, 423,000 hectares of land were distributed between 1922 and 1925. Kasulaitis quotes the great Italian Christian Democrat Alcide De Gasperi strongly praising the land reform of Father Krupavičius and the Party.

With the United States approaching its bicentennial, one could only hope that the American Founding Fathers would have been as farsighted as the Lithuanians in fostering economic democracy. True, land was distributed quite freely — mainly because there was so much of it — but America had other economic institutions which were soon to corrupt its political democracy. Leaders such as Thomas Jefferson, Albert Gallatin, and Samuel Adams recognized the threat of concentrations of wealth.

According to historian Eric Foner, during 1778 and 1779, Samuel Adams, as a member of Congress, condemned the "spirit of avarice" among businessmen who were more interested in a "monopoly of Trade" than "the liberty of their country." According to Foner, "during the American Revolution, countless communities established popular committees to regulate prices and profits. Adams felt such activities were "wise and salutary." Foner quotes Adams, "If the popular indignation can once be raised to a suitable pitch as I think it can, it will become dangerous for them to withhold their goods or demand an exorbitant price for them. ... I thing every step should be taken for the downfall of such wretches."

Albert Gallatin, later to be Secretary of the Treasury in the Presidential Administrations of Thomas Jefferson and James Madison, wrote in 1797, "The democratic principle on which this nation was founded should not be restricted to the political process but should be applied to the industrial operation as well."

Thomas Jefferson, President from 1801 to 1809, wrote to Logan in 1816, "I hope we shall... crush in its birth the aristocracy of our moneyed corporations, which dare already to challenge our government to a trial of strength and bid defiance to the laws of our country."

Unfortunately, these men and others could not convince enough of their contemporaries to write into the U.S. Constitution clauses or amendments guaranteeing economic democracy. Now, the United States begins its third century facing the ugly consequences of that omission. Possibly, Lithuanian Christian Democrats in the United States can help it overcome this injustice — with the same wisdom and courage their forebears used in Lithuania in the first quarter of this century.

One of the ironies of history is that the first Central Committee of the Lithuanian Christian Democratic Party was organized in June, 1917 in St. Petersburg (Petrograd, then, Leningrad) by Lithuanian immigrants and refugees. It is unfortunate these Christian Democrats were not able to influence the Bolsheviks who made their first of two attempts to seize the Russian government in the same city only a few weeks later — July 16-18. The second attempt — November 7th — succeeded. Possibly, with Lithuanians leading the way, Christian Democracy will finally be the salvation of Russia.

One final comment. In "Part V, Profiles in Action: The Leaders of an Era" or Chapters 15 and 16, the author identifies some of the outstanding Christian Democrats.

It is good he has done this, for two reasons. The first is the Christian meaning of what it is to be a leader.

Jesus teaches, "He who is greatest among you shall be your servant;" (Matthew 23:11). Again He says, "If any one would be first, he must be last of all and servant of all." (Mark 9:35). Jesus uses the analogy of a shepherd to describe a true leader. "I am the good shepherd. The good shepherd lays down his life for his sheep. He who is a hireling and not a shepherd, whose own the sheep are not, sees the wolf coming and leaves the sheep and flees; and the wolf snatches them and scatters them." (John 10:11, 12). Lithuanian Christian Democrats noted here approached this leadership ideal of "servant" and "shepherd."

The second reason it is good that Kasulaitis adequately identifies outstanding Christian Democrats is because democracy cannot be founded or perpetuated without these kinds of leaders. Jacques Maritain in his *Man and the State* explains this reality well.

> The last issue to be discussed no longer deals with the people, but with — how shall I designate them? — well, with the inspired servants or prophets of the people.
>
> What I mean is that it is not enough to define a democratic society by its legal srtucture. Another element plays also a basic part, namely the dynamic leaven or energy which fosters political movement, and which cannot be inscribed in any constitution or embodied in any institution, since it is both personal and contingent in nature, and rooted in free initiative. I should like to call that existential factor a prophetic factor. Democracy cannot do without it. The people need prophets.

And those servants or prophets of the people are not — not necessarily — elected representatives of the people. This mission starts in their own hearts and consciousness. In this sense they are self-appointed prophets. They are needed in the normal functioning of a democratic society. They are needed especially in the periods of crisis, birth, or basic renewal of a democratic society. (Maritain, Jacques; *Man and the State;* Univeristy of Chicago Press, Chicago, Illinois, 1951, page 139).

Many of the Founding Fathers of Lithuania, as well as of the United States, can be called servants and prophets of the people. We need these same kind of persons today and in the future. *Lithuanian Christian Democracy* by Algirdas Kasulaitis helps us appreciate this.

Richard Giloth
Director, The Christian Democratic Center
Chairman, Christian Democratic movement
of the United States

II

Around the year 1880, European politics shifted toward social reform. Christians did not trust the expanding doctrine of materialism so they set up their own social movements which developed into Christian political parties.

Lithuanian Christian Democracy played a major role in Lithuania after World War I, when it called for new aims in re-building Lithuania, agreeing that economic policy is basic, but insisting that it should not be stressed at the expense of political and cultural policy.

It is the nature of all wars to destroy the world as it is, to a greater or lesser degree. World War One was the most important in the destruction of many empires and dynasties, the systems by which so much of the world had been governed for so long.

Let us go back to the year of 1918, more than half a century ago, when the history of the world began to assume a new shape.

To the country of Lithuania it was an exhilarating period of its political and physical renewal — rising as if from the grave — emerging again as an independent nation after 120 years of suppression and national degradation by Russia.

Lithuania, regained its independence in 1918 as a small nation, ruminating on its ancient struggle for freedom when the Kingdom of Lithuania was established in 1253, happily recalling the acceptance of Christianity by the country in 1387, and gaining strength in recalling the greatness of the past when under Vytautas the Great, the lands reached from the Baltic Sea on the North to the Black Sea on the South; and staunchly determined that Christian principles of tolerance and religious freedom prevail as in the official Code of Laws, the "statutes of Lithuania", published in 1548. This was the first book of laws published in Europe.

So great is the acceleration of change in our times, that it is suggested that the world only ten years hence will be almost totally different in character and texture. We stop and ask, "Will it?" "Why?" What different values will hold in a "new" world? Will the spiritual values be different as well as the political and material? What separates the past from today?

The answers profoundly affect us all. The unthinkable alternatives are, alas, all too thinkable!

Notwithstanding the ultimate aims of politics, the survival of a small nation is imposssible if a larger nation by brutal aggrandizement accompanied by tricky documents "clearly" perform the annihilation of a country and the extinction of a people.

The United States is known to be the Champion of Democracy. Yet, today, we find it two-faced in its Foreign Policy. From the time of President Roosevelt the Administration states and re-states that it does not acknowledge the forced occupation of Lithuania, Latvia and Estonia in 1940 by the imperialistic powers of Communist Russia. It confirms that the United States supports and will continue to support the humanitarian principles of self determination and freedom to all peoples, and recognizes Lithuania's claim to independence.

We depend upon and trust our United States government because it is the so-called Champion of Democracy, but we must raise our voices against the trickery of the signing of the Helsinki Pact, with the use of a "new" word, "detente".

How can the United States condone aggressive conquest with one hand and condemn it with the other? While nations throughout the world are re-asserting their identities, the U.S.A. and the U.S.S.R. are considered as bartering away the freedom and sovereignty of other nations. Why must larger powers surreptitiously gobble up small nations, refusing them the right to life with their customs and cultures in their own lands? What possible threat can a small nation present to a "goliath"?

It is inconceivable that the United States could lend endorsement to penurious agreements and pledge faith with a government brutally subjugating other nations.

No group or power has the moral right to sign away or speak away the rights of another nation. We remind our powers that there is extreme danger that ultimately our own United States can become the sacrifice.

We must turn to the study of Christian Democratic principles and practices. We need courage and wisdom to return to humane ideas and practices. We need mature minds with respect and love for our fellow man, and men in government who will seek the light of the Christian way — to transform the world into a place where men and their world work in harmony instead of against each other. This may be the hardest problem we have yet to face.

ANTHONY J. RUDIS

INTRODUCTION

Looking back to Lithuania's recent past when the nation was free, and having personal recollections of the important national leaders, we are aware that Lithuania of that time was democratic and her leaders were deeply committed, idealistic democrats. The secret of Lithuania's progress after the country regained her freedom in 1918 and started an independent life under severe political and economic conditions, was the nation's adherence to true democratic principles. Lithuanian population remained deeply democratic even later when the government of the rebuilt and progressive country fell into non-democratic hands.

Presently, the term "democracy" is universally popular. The name is being used even by those political systems, groups and individuals who neither understand what democracy is nor seek to espouse it. These sources are dangerous to true democracy. Society which does not fully understand what true democracy is, is in danger of assuming that all the errors perpetrated in its name by various political systems, groups, or individuals are inherent in the principles of democracy, and consequently may turn away from it.

Democracy is a societal concern embracing all of society's multitudinous spheres, especially those activities and people who are in need of more help of one kind or another than others.

A democrat is a person who is conscious of his and his fellow man's responsibilities and rights, and concerns himself with the well-being of the whole society.

Democratic society is distinguished by its societal consciousness, manifesting itself by solidarity of action seeking the well-being of all, especially those whose needs are more acute.

Democratic system and government is distinguished by its concern for the well-being and rights of all citizens, especially those who need outside help the most. In those instances where governmental concerns are limited to one group or members of one political party, where some are exploited and some privileged, as is the case presently in the communist countries, democracy is replaced by a group or a party hegemony for the purpose of exploiting the citizenry for the benefit of a small group of its followers.

The results of democratic tendencies and activities are very much dependent on the ideological underpinnings of the society on the whole. Understanding the nature of man, the ultimate goals of life, gradation of values, and personal, familial, societal, moral principles are of great importance to democracy's concept. It is, therefore, hard to imagine that true democracy can be sustained by atheistic forces under any name, simply because their beliefs about the nature of man, ultimate goal of life and values are in error. According to Pope Leo XIII, "the well-being of a state depends on the fact by what religion God is worshipped" (Immortale Dei). This very precept applies also to democracy: in the several countries of the world, democratic action depends on the principles by which a country lives — governs its life, what gods it worships.

Christian Democracy as the very term implies, is based on the principles of Christian doctrine. A true Christian Democracy is an activity by Christian-inspired people seeking societal well-being in a Christian way. In such democratic system, the government, as well as, every citizen, lives by the same principles, does not usurp societal prerogatives or initiatives. Christian Democracy does not seek centralization of power through nationalization, but concerns itself with the upgrading of citizens' initiatives and their active participation in societal life.

Although in theory all citizens are equal, in real life some of society's members are less fortunate — the poor, the disabled, the least educated. The government and society must show more concern for them and to raise their well-being. Any country is as democratic as it seeks (and how it goes about) in achieving this most important goal.

It must be understood that true perception of democracy does not automatically manifest itself in individual mind or societal life. Humanity needs a constant educational process to absorb democratic precepts.

Both from the philosophical point of view and from the historical experiences of nations, it seems that the world and the several countries will be only as happy as they will embrace Christian Democracy. In the same vein, Lithuania's future when she regains her independence, (and the future of other nations), will to a great degree depend upon the values and maturization process of their future generations.

MOST REV. V. BRIZGYS

PREFACE

The history of Lithuanian Christian Democracy spans more than a century. It also embraces the most interesting period in Lithuania's road from an occupied country to a modern, independent Republic. It is marked by tragedy and triumph, by suffering and achievement, by lost battles and glorious victories. It is mostly a story of people dedicated to the single-minded task of self-determination. In this long and ultimately successful struggle, Lithuanian Christian Democrats played a key role. The Christian Democratic Party was in power only a short period of time, but its achievements permeated the whole fiber of politics in Lithuania and served as a solid basis upon which the people built a remarkable national structure.

This booklet is not intended to be an exhaustive study of Lithuanian Christian Democracy. (Without source material, which at this time is denied Lithuanian writers, any substantive in-depth study is quite impossible). Its modest aim is simply to present to the Lithuanian

XX

friends an outline of Christian Democratic history in Lithuania: its main historic points, trials and tribulations, achievements and goals.

I do intend to follow-up this study with a paper on the development of Lithuanian Christian Democratic thought; its primary sources, ideological underpinnings, developmental periods, etc.

I'm pleased to acknowledge here my debt to many friends for their encouragement and aid in preparation of this study. I'm especially grateful to H.E. Bishop Vincentas Brizgys, A. Garka, Mrs. O. Žilinskas, P. Razgaitis, Dr. B. Gidžiūnas, O.F.M., former Editor of "Tėvynės Sargas" Dr. Domas Jasaitis, Secretary of the Central Committee of LCDU Adomas Viliušis and others for their valuable suggestions. Publications Commission of the Leo XIII Fund deserves a warm and personal thanks for its constant help. I owe a special debt to the Executive Committee of Leo XIII Fund and all the Sponsors (whose names are listed elswhere in the book) for its and their generosity. Finally, this study would have never been completed without the help of my wife, whose contribution is immeasurable.

Lithuania is again in bondage; occupied, enslaved, and exploited by the cruel imperialistic power of the Soviet Union. The brave nation is again waging a relentless struggle for freedom and independence. Christian Democracy is again in the midst of this national endeavor. If anything, these short pages bear witness to the fact that Lithuania and Lithuanian Christian Democracy will not only survive — it will prevail.

A. J. K.

Cleveland
October 1, 1975

MARIA RUDIS

ANTHONY J. RUDIS

The Leo XIII Fund is grateful to *Mr. and Mrs. An thony J. Rudis* of Chicago, Ill. whose generous contribution of $1,000 was of great help in defraying the cost of preparation and publishing this study. This is but one example of their great generosity to various Lithuanian affairs and undertakings.

Anthony J. Rudis, 64, is one of the most prominent leaders of the substantial American-Lithuanian community. He is a long-time member of the governing bodies of the American-Lithuan'an Council (its Chairman in 1965-1967), Lithuanian Roman Catholic Federation (its President in 1961-1964 and again in 1965-1967), Lithuanian Roman Catholic Alliance of America, Lithuanian Chamber of Commerce (its President in 1951-1966), and others. He was also a special advisor to Rep. Charles J. Kersten, Chairman of the Baltic Committee of the U.S. House of Representatives, prime fund-raiser for Maria High School in Chicago, the Church of the Nativity of the Blessed Virgin Mary, the Lithuanian Marian Fathers' Monastery, and the Lithuanian daily "Draugas" office building.

Mr. Rudis is also a member of the Chicago Association of Commerce and Industry, Illinois Manufacturers' Association, Chicago Council on Foreign Relations, as well as, founder of the American Immigration Museum, and the Lithuanian Radio Forum.

Of Lithuanian parentage Mr. Rudis is a graduate of the Illinois Institute of Technology with a degree in mechanical engineering. He is the founder (in 1942) and President of the Rockwell Engineering Company in Chicago.

Maria Rudis, also of Lithuanian descent, is similarly active in Lithuanian affairs in leadership positions. A graduate of de Paul University Mrs. Rudis is active in the company affairs, co-producer of the Lithuanian Radio Forum, long-time Director and presently National Chairwoman of the United Lithuanian Relief Fund of America. An engaging public speaker, Mrs. Rudis addressed numerous American and foreign audiences on Lithuanian subjects. She also sponsored several nationwide Lithuanian cultural symposia, as well as, song and folk dance festivals.

LEO XIII FUND IS GRATEFUL TO THE FOLLOWING SPONSORS WHOSE GENEROUS CONTRIBUTIONS HELPED MAKE THE PUBLICATION OF THIS STUDY POSSIBLE.

$ 150 **Contributors:** Pr. Razgaitis, Seven Hills, Ohio.

$ 100 **Contributors:** **A.** Garka, Euclid, Ohio, **J. L. Giedraitis**, East Northport, N. Y., **H. Idzelis**, Cleveland, Ohio, **Rev. B. Ivanauskas**, Cleveland, Ohio, **Prof. Dr. P. Jucaitis**, Rocky River, Ohio, V. Juodis, Cleveland, Ohio, **Mr. and Mrs. J. Kunevičius**, Parma, Ohio, J. **Meškauskas, M.D.**, Chicago, Ill., **A. Pautienis**, Cleveland Hts., Ohio, **Elena Repšys, D.D.S.**, Chicago, Ill., **Mrs. M. Šmulkštys**, Evanston, Ill., J. **Starkus, M.D.**, Chicago, Ill., **P. Spetyla**, Chicago, Ill., **A.** Styra, Cleveland, Ohio, **P. Tamulionis**, Cleveland, Ohio, **Dr. J. K. Valiūnas**, Rochelle, N. Y., **X.Y.**, Euclid, Ohio.

$ 75 **Contributors:** Rev. A. Goldikovskis, Cleveland, Ohio.

$ 50 **Contributors:** St. Alšėnas, Brecksville, Ohio, Msgr. P. M. Juras, A. P., O.F.M., Putnam, Conn., P. Kliorys, South Euclid, Ohio, Rev. Vac. Martinkus, Providence, R.I., M. Ž., Cleveland Hts., Ohio.

$ 30 **Contributors:** Rev. J. Čekavičius, Jamaica, N. Y., V. Jokubaitis, Cleveland, Ohio, Aldona Rugis, M.D., Chicago, Ill., P. Skardis, Euclid, Ohio, P. Zigmantas, Richmond Hts., Ohio.

$ 25 **Contributors:** J. Balbatas, Cleveland, Ohio, Msgr. Vyt. Balčiūnas, Thompson, Conn., A. Balčytis, Chicago, Ill., Msgr. J. Balkūnas, A.P., Maspeth, N.Y., R. Bridžius, Cleveland, Ohio, B.B., Southgate, Mich., P. Gruodis, Chicago, Ill., K.V. J. Lyndhurst, Ohio, Alf. Karklius, Bratenahl, Ohio, Prof. B. J. Kaslas, Wyoming, Pa., Dr. P. Kazlas, Hot Springs, Ark., Rt. Rev. Msgr. J. A. Kučingis, Los Angeles, Cal., Dr. Eng. J. Kuodis, Arlington, Mass., Lith. Cath. Religious Aid, Maspeth, N. Y., LCDU Cleveland, Ohio, Chapter, Lithuanian Jesuit Fathers in Cleveland, Ohio, P. Maldeikis, Phoenix, Ariz., A. Masilionis, Cleveland, Ohio, K. Mickevičius, Chicago, Ill., P. Mikšys, Juno Beach, Florida, Msgr. V. Mincevičius, Roma, Italy, P. Minkūnas, Woodhaven, N. Y., K. Pabedinskas, Oak Park, Ill., J. Paškus, Chicago, Ill., K. Povilaitis, Chicago, Ill., Pr. Povilaitis, Evergreen Park, Ill., St. Rauckinas, Chicago, Ill., Rev. Dr. C. Širvaitis, Holland, Pa., Vl. Šoliūnas, Willow Springs, Ill., A. Tamulionis, Bratenahl, Ohio, Pr. Vainauskas, Brooklyn, N. Y., Ad. Viliušis, Chicago, Ill., A. B. Žukauskas, Hinsdale, Ill., B. Žukauskas, Chicago, Ill.

PART I

LITHUANIA:
A PROFILE

1

PHYSIOGRAPHY

Position. Lithuania is southeastern basin country of the Baltic Sea, actually Nemunas basin country. Geographically it is located in Central Europe or Balto-Scandinavian region.[1]

Area. Lithuania covers 33,900 square miles[2] of land (including the Klaipėda and Vilnius regions, which some sources leave out simply because at one time these territories were temporarily occupied by foreign powers). Ethnographic boundaries of Lithuania are even larger. Thus, Lithuania is somewhat larger than Switzerland, Belgium or Denmark.[3]

Surface. Geological surface of Lithuania is of glacial origin. Ice Age glaciers moving from Scandinavia covered Lithuanian territory with moraines of various depths. The surface was finally formed by flowing waters, which performed drainage job and formed the present hydrographical network. The largest river is Nemunas (578 miles).[4]

ŠIAULIAI

PANEVĖŽYS

KLAIPĖDA

KAUNAS

VILNIUS

GARDINAS

LITHUANIA, THE GATEWAY BETWEEN WEST AND EAST

EUROPE

ATLANTIC OCEAN

NORTH AFRICA

Climate. Lithuania belongs to the Middle European climate belt in the transitory zone between Europe's oceanic and continental climate. The annual mean temperature is 43° Fahrenheit.[5]

Flora. From the botanical point of view, Lithuania belongs to the "variety" forest zones. At present, the evergreens are predominant (pine and fir trees). The forests cover about 23 percent of the territory.[6]

Wildlife. In general, it is the same as in the rest of Middle Europe. Mooses are the largest wild animals. Over 250 different types of birds spend the summer or the whole year in Lithuania.

Boundaries. Lithuania's northern boundary with Latvia dates from the XIIIth century and was only slightly altered by a treaty in 1921. Eastern boundary with the Soviet Union was established in 1920 by the Peace Treaty of Moscow. Western boundary with Germany was established in 1928 by a treaty. It must be noted, however, that this boundary falls way short of the true ethnographic boundary and the western boundary still awaits a definite and just establishment. The southern boundary with Poland has never actually been established to the satisfaction of rightful Lithuanian claims.[7]

POPULATION

At the end of 1939, Lithuania had a population of 3,200,000.[1] Under normal conditions, present day Lithuania should have ca. 4,500,000 inhabitants. According to present Soviet statistics, it has only slightly over 3,000,000. The loss of population according to knowledgeable demographers is due primarily to Soviet and Nazi genocidical practices. The losses of population are calculated as follows:

First Soviet occupation	(1940-1941)	60,000
German occupation	(1941-1944)	250,000
Second Soviet occupation	(since 1944)	570,000
Refugess		280,000
	TOTAL	1,160,000[2]

RELIGION

In 1938, 85 percent of the population were Roman Catholics, 7 percent Jewish, 2.3 percent Greek Orthodox, 4.2 percent Protestant, and 1.5 percent others.[3]

LANGUAGE

The Lithuanian language is a completely separate and distinct branch of the Indo-European family of languages. It is one of the oldest living tongues greatly admired by philologists, as well as a modern language spoken by more than 4,000,000 people. It differs completely from Slavic or Germanic languages.

Together with Latvian and old Prussian languages (the latter now extinct) and some also extinct dialects, which comprise the Baltic language group, Lithuanian has its roots in the ancient Proto-Baltic. After the Proto-Baltic divided (ca. IV - III century B.C.) the Eastern part split again into Lithuanian and Latvian (ca. VIII century A.D.). Since then both languages developed in similar, yet separate ways.

The first written document in Lithuania dates back to the very beginning of the XVI century. First substantial texts date back to mid-sixteenth century and are of religious character, written in several Lithuanian dialects.

As a living thing the Lithuanian language through the centuries changed substantially. It lost some of its older characteristics and forms. Slavic influence was at times strong and prolonged. (Less so Germanic influence). Thousands of Slavic words found their way into several Lithuanian dialects. However, these borrowings never

6

cluttered the Standard Lithuanian.[4] The latter evolved from the southwestern subdialect of Lithuanian mostly because of the need of uniformity for the written language.[5]

However, Lithuanian is still "the most archaic among all the Indo-European languages spoken today, and as a result is very useful, indeed, indispensible in the study of Indo - European linguistics".[6] The same opinion was and is expressed by many other noted philologists: P. Ruhig, J. Vater, von Bohlen, W. Humboldt, J. Karlowicz, August Schleicher, Benjamin D. Dwight, Elise Reclus.[7]

"Finally, the famous philosopher Immanuel Kant in the preface to his Lithuanian Grammar writes: 'She (Lithuania) must be preserved, for her tongue possesses the key which opens the enigmas not only of philology but of history'." [8]

3

HISTORICAL OUTLINE

The Lithuanian people are of Indo-European race and live, since time immemorial, on the shores of the Baltic Sea.[1] The Roman Historian Tacitus (II century A.D.) cites the Lithuanians under the denomination of "aestiorum gentes", who were "gens humanissima". A clearer picture of the Lithuanians emerges only in the IX and X centuries, but written history of Lithuania starts in the early XIII century.

From the beginning, Lithuanians had to struggle with the Order of Teutonic Knights of Saint Mary, a Germanic, monastic, as well as, a military order founded in Palestine during the Crusades. When the Christians were driven out of Asia Minor, the Order settled in Prussia, conquered its Lithuanian population and began its expansion towards other Lithuanian territories. In this quest, the Order received aid from all European countries.

For a century and a half, the Knights tried in vain to beat the Lithuanians into submission. The Order proclaimed that they were fighting the "Saracens of the North" with the sole intention of Christianizing them. Help flowed from every Christian nation. But to no avail. Lithuanians fought bravely, and this period is full of heroism, glorious victories, and stunning defeats.

In the middle of the XIII century, Lithuania was already a well organized state under Grand Duke Mindaugas.[2] In 1251 Mindaugas was baptized[3] and two years later crowned by the Pontiff as King of Lithuania.

During her struggle with the Teutonic Knights, Lithuania was blessed with a succession of brilliant leaders who not only resisted the Order, but at the same time, continuously expanded the empire eastward. In the XIV and XV centuries, Lithuania became the most powerful empire in Middle and Eastern Europe. During the reign of Vytautas the Great[4] (1392 - 1430), the boundaries of Lithuania reached from the Baltic to the Black Sea. Jogaila,[5] a cousin of Vytautas the Great, occupied the royal throne of Poland and his dynasty reigned in Poland for nearly 200 years.

The Lithuanians were heathens until the XIV century. By this time, every European country was Christian. Most of the Russian tribes living within Lithuanian borders were also Christian of Orthodox faith, and influenced by the culture of the Byzantine Empire.

Several grand dukes of Lithuania thought about Christianity. However, they were never impressed by the rigid eastern culture and, even less impressed by Christianity represented by the militaristic and land-hungry Teutonic Knights.

9

Lithuania became Christian in 1387 when King Jogaila of Poland and Vytautas the Great embraced Christianity.

In 1410, Vytautas the Great, with the help of Jogaila, decisively beat the Order in the Battle of Tannenberg, which never again recovered or menaced Lithuania and her neighbors.[6]

Having resolved this problem, Lithuania found herself settled with another. When Jogaila accepted the throne of Poland (and became Wladislaw II), he was still the Grand Duke of Lithuania. This personal union was objectionable to Lithuanians and finally Jogaila gave up the title. Vytautas the Great became the Chief-of-State in name as well as in fact.

The idea of personal union, however, did not die in Poland. After the Death of Vytautas the Great, who left no heirs, Lithuanians elected as their Grand Duke, the younger son of King Jogaila, Kazimieras, whose brother by that time took his father's place as the King of Poland. When he suddenly died, the Poles immediately elected Kazimieras as their King. The personal union was again established and the Poles maintained it until the end of Jogaila's dynasty. (Every time a Polish King would die, Poland would elect the then Grand Duke of Lithuania to be her King.)

This personal union with Poland proved to be misfortunate. The kings usually resided in Poland and the Lithuanian affairs suffered. This coupled with the rise of the Russian State spelled trouble for Lithuania. The nobility gained more and more power, accepted Polish culture and started to care more about their own affairs than those of the country.

The nobility, to be sure, never wanted any union with Poland. However, in their thirst for personal power and privileges, they compromised to a point where in 1569, by the Treaty of Lublin, Lithuania and Poland formally united into one Commonwealth. It was never a single state, but a loose confederation with one king. Otherwise, both countries were separate states to the end.

However, even this type of a union proved to be disadvantageous to Lithuania. Following the Polish nobility, Lithuanian aristocracy grabbed as much power as possible. The King's power slowly, but surely, deteriorated. Ever-increasing power also corrupted the nobility. Under these conditions, it was only a matter of time before the more powerful neighbors conquered both states. Thus, in 1795, Lithuania fell to the Russians, to rise again only after more than a century under quite a different set of conditions.[7]

PART II

CHRISTIAN DEMOCRACY:
A FORCE OF PROGRESS

4

POLITICAL, SOCIAL AND ECONOMIC CONDITIONS IN THE XIX CENTURY

The end of the XVIII century meant also the end of the Lithuanian-Polish Commonwealth. After the second Russian invasion (during the Northern Wars — 1701-1721) the armies of Peter the Great failed to withdraw to Russia. Sizable units stayed in the Commonwealth's territory. This fifth column only hastened the disintegration of the Commonwealth. Decaying from within, powerless and helpless, it was finally partitioned between Russia, Prussia, and Austria in 1772, 1793 and 1795. Most of Lithuania fell under Russian control. An Iron Curtain, not unlike the Iron Curtain of today, descended around Lithuania and it was to lift only after 123 years of a most severe and cruel occupation and exploitation.

Enduring as it was, Russian domination was never accepted by the Lithuanians as the final solution of their fate. They fought almost incessantly, and used all possible means to rid themselves of the despised tyranny of Czarist Russia.

The resistance was by no means easy. On the one hand, Russian occupation was extremely harsh and very cruel, and, on the other, the social, economic, and cultural conditions within Lithuania were far from ideal to wage a systematic, well-organized, and continuous resistance.

Imperialistic Russia, whose territories Lithuania once ruled with benevolence and great political wisdom, was determined to end the life of Lithuania once and for all. To this end, Russia employed all classic tools of tyranny.

To erace any trace of Lithuanian identity, even the name "Lithuania" was forbidden and it was substituted by the bland "Northwestern Country" title. Every executive, political, and administrative position was given to Russian officials, especially imported from Russia. (This included even the county level.) All available land was sold to numerous Russian colonists who flocked to Lithuania to start a fortune, a new life, or a new career. In 1832, the famous University of Vilnius, for decades the center of higher learning in all East Central Europe, and the heart of Lithuanian culture, was closed. In 1840, the Lithuania Statute, one of the truly great legal documents of the XVI century Europe, was abolished and replaced by Russian Law.[1] The Lithuanian language was forbidden in schools. In 1864, the government of St. Petersburg outlawed the printing of any Lithuanian books and periodicals in Latin characters.

Especially hard hit was the Catholic Church. Not unlike Communist Kremlin, the imperialist St. Petersburg saw in the Catholic Church the main adversary of its devious schemes, and rightly so. To silence it, the imperial government used extremely harsh methods. Several dozen of the Catholic churches were confiscated and reopened as Russian Orthodox Churches. Priests were forbidden to leave the boundaries of their parishes on any matter. Bishops were hindered in administration of their dioceses. Sermons were censored and only those approved were allowed to be preached. Candidates for the priesthood were carefully screened and only those with government approval were allowed to enter theological seminaries. The slightest infraction by the religious of the myriad of rules was punishable by exile to the Siberian labor camps. These rules, as a matter of policy, were very closely adhered to.

Such severe occupational policy, however, did not extinguish the hope of freedom. During the long decades of virtual slavery Lithuanians mounted no less than four armed and bloody rebellions. Alas, none too successful.

The first insurrection was mounted by Thadeus Kosciuszko in 1794, even before the third partition of Lithuania by Russia, Prussia and Austria. It was an attempt to regain freedom and territories lost to Russia in the two previous partitions of 1772 and 1793. Skirmishes and battles with the much more powerful Russian garrisons took place in many corners of Lithuania. Most major cities were liberated as the revolt spread throughout the country. However, the ultimate victory belonged to the oppressors. First Lithuanian and later joint Lithuanian-Polish insurgents were beaten. The final partition of both countries followed in 1795. A 123 year Russian tyrrany in Lithuania had begun.[2]

The second opportunity arose in 1812, during Napoleon's march to Moscow. Nine regiments of Lithuanian volunteers fought the Russians in the hope of regaining freedom.

The third insurrection broke out in 1831 on a much larger scale. Thousands of insurgents fought brilliant battles and for a time, the whole etnographic Lithuania was again in their hands. However, they were unable to overpower either Vilnius or Kaunas (both largest cities in Lithuania), and this proved to be the insurrection's downfall.[3]

The Lithuanians revolted for the fourth time in 1863, in the most powerful attempt yet to rid themselves of the hated Russians. For eighteen months battles raged throughout the length and breadth of the land. As on previous occasions, Russian power proved to be more than equal to the poorly armed volunteer forces. The insurrection was crushed mercilessly.[4]

The fifth insurrection occurred in 1905 and was of a quite different character. Instead of arms, the power of petition was used and quite successfully. No small role was played by different circumstances enveloping the Russian empire. Russo-Japanese War and the concurrent revolution within the empire was not lost on the Czarist government. A thaw was indicated and in its wake, some of the Lithuanian demands were met. However, yet another decade passed before Lithuania finally rid herself of the century-old yoke of foreign domination.

The spirit of freedom and the resultant insurrections were but a part of a greater and deeper change in the soul of the nation.

One of the basic social characteristics of XIX century Lithuania was the final Polonization of the Lithuanian nobility. The demoralization of the ruling class began with the establishment of the Lithuanian-Polish Commonwealth. The Lithuanian nobility, rich but powerless in an absolute monarchy of the Lithuanian Grand-Duchy, was very much impressed by the quasi-parliamentary system of Poland where the nobility enjoyed wide privileges and a good measure of power. This example was not lost on their Lithuanian counterparts. The growing power of Moscow during the XVI century drew both countries closer together in a natural military cooperation. However, cooperation did not end there. As fortunes of the country sagged and the sovereign needed more and more help, the nobility quickly learned the game of give and take. The appetite for more power and greater privileges grew even faster during the Commonwealth years. With the gradual decay of the state, the nobility acquired almost complete power, and at the same time, more of the Polish cultural and national characteristics. This process measurably accelerated during the Russian occupation.

Alienation of the nobility from the common people did not particularly effect the relatively free minority of the townsmen. However, the vast majority of the population — the peasantry, was completely enslaved in the process. On the one hand, the tyranny of Russia was harsh, on the other, the natural leaders of the populous were not only completely alienated from the common people but continued to keep them in absolute servitude. This undoubtedly was the darkest period in the long history of the country. In the end, however, it proved to be the channel through which the country not only moved out of bondage, but also into a modern, social, economic, and political system.

Serfdom was the basic characteristic of XIX century Lithuania for several reasons: First, it enveloped the vast majority of the population. Second, it degenerated into virtual slavery and reached the limits of human endurance.[5] And, third, it served as an impetus for the country to change its destiny once and for all. To brake with the past; to stand on its own feet; to be the master of its own fate. There was really no other way, because there was nothing to be lost anymore. National freedom was lost and Russia was the unquestioned master of the land. The nobility had no ties with the people. The economic and social conditions were intolerable.

Servitude was not of Lithuanian origin. It was imported from outside together with the privileges and powers of the nobility. Nevertheless, it took extreme forms. After Lithuania was absorbed by Russia, the peasant had lost every political, economic, and human right.

The government exerted all power to change the peasantry's very soul. To Russianize the population, St. Petersburg outlawed the Lithuanian language in schools and later prohibited all printing in Latin characters. Catholicism was discouraged and the Church persecuted, while Russian Orthodox was highly favored. Russian was instituted as the offical language of the country. All organizations and meetings were forbidden.

On top of that, the serf was under complete control of his master. The latter, commanded not only the peasant's labor services but his pay, freedom of movement, recreation and schooling, etc. The landlord was the only and ultimate judge and from his sentence there was no appeal. There were instances when serfs were actually bought or exchanged like so many goods.

At this point the Lithuanian peasant struck back.

5

THE FIRST SEEDS OF
CHRISTIAN DEMOCRACY

As mentioned elsewhere, the struggle for national freedom and human rights was not limited to armed rebellion. It was waged in several directions and was led by a new breed of leaders.

Among all the misfortunes of the XIX century, the bright spot was the emergence of a nucleus of educated people of common stock. As the number of these educated commoners increased, many of them did not sever their ties with the peasantry, but joined them in their struggle for national identity. Because of their education, they quite naturally assumed the positions of leadership vacated by the Polonized nobility. They were the first of the new breed of genuine leaders who eventually changed the destiny of the country.

Some of them were also the first sowers of Christian Democratic seeds. Tender as those seeds were, they found a fertile soil and later grew into a powerful movement.

These first seeds of Christian Democratic thought were transplanted from Western Europe where unbridled liberal capitalism and ever-increasing materialism gave birth to new social and economic doctrines. Among them, Christian Democracy, slowly but surely, emerged as a genuinely progressive force.

One of the first Christian Democratic forerunners was the *Reverend Antanas Strazdas* (1763 - 1833).[1] Father Strazdas was a commoner by birth and during the turn of the century, one of the few educated people among commoners. No intellectual, Father Strazdas was, however, a man of letters and action. His most important characteristics were his love for everything Lithuanian and his friendship with the peasantry. His most powerful weapon in his struggle with the Russians and with mostly Polonized clergy, was his songs. A poet of considerable talent, Father Strazdas' songs were mostly written and composed for the common people. In them, the poet not only captured the troubles and tribulations of the dreary lives of the serfs, but also mixed in a good dose of satire directed straight at the nobility: its denationalization, degeneration, moral laxity, etc. These songs became immensely popular amongst the peasantry and brightened many a heart.

In private life, a simple and unassuming man, Father Strazdas, would not shy away from a good fight, especially if it concerned the common man and his rights. For this, he was many times punished by his ecclesiastical superiors in whose eyes any good word for serfs was an indiscretion to say the very least. The last five years of his life he spent mostly as a farmer, just like the people he so dearly loved and worked for.

21

Another forerunner of Christian Democratic thought was poet and linguist *Bishop Antanas Baranauskas* (1831 - 1902).[2] He too was of common stock although his parents were free small landowners. As a Bishop of Seinai, he was a model shepherd. At the time when no educated Lithuanian dared to speak Lithuanian in public, Bishop Baranauskas was the first to preach in his native tongue. As a poet, Bishop Baranauskas was unsurpassed at that time. In his religious and other poetry, he not only underscored the beauty of the Lithuanian language, but also the pride of Lithuanian nationality.

Father Antanas Vienažindys (1841-1892)[3] became influential also mainly on the strength of his poetry. A talented lyric poet, he concentrated his attention in describing the harsh reality of serfdom. Many of his poems became songs and had a tremendous influence in raising the spirit of the common people.

There were others, clergy and laymen alike, who in the same vein struggled for Lithuania, the common man, and the Church.

This period, lasting until about 1850, could be called *Missionary Period.*[4] The small group of patriots, mostly priests of common birth, were by no means Christian Democrats as we understand them in today's context. (As a matter of fact, the very term Christian Democracy first appeared in print only some fifty years later.) However, their actions and their writings, under the circumstances, were of tremendous importance to the masses, desperately seeking their own identity and struggling to alleviate social, political, economic, and religious bondage. In this sense, this small group of outstanding men were like the prophets of old who led the Israelites to the Promised

Bishop Antanas Baranauskas

Land. Their actions and their writings were permeated by genuine social concern for the suppressed peasantry, by deep Christian faith and by true Lithuanian self-conciousness.

In their own way, they paved the road for the Christian Democratic action which could be well called the *Period of Reform of the Peasantry*.[5] This period lasted about thirty years and was dominated by one of the greatest Lithuanians of the century, *Bishop Motiejus Valančius* (1801-1875).[6]

When Bishop Valančius became ordinary of the Varniai[7] diocese in 1850, Lithuania was again on a collision course with the Czarist regime. The preceding half century did not bring any changes to the oppressed peasantry, let alone basic changes. The insurrection of 1831 failed and in its aftermath the conditions all but worsened. However, change from within was in the wind, precipitated by the small group of social minded and intensely patriotic priests.

In his early ecclesiastical career, young Father Valančius was a diligent priest and a gifted teacher. Traveling through different schools in Russia and Lithuania, he keenly observed not only the deplorable conditions of the peasantry, but also the budding Lithuanian movement. Although himself a son of a well-to-do free landowner, he early identified himself with the vast majority of serfs and their plight. A compassionate man, he was also a man of letters and action. These qualities made him a natural leader, and he accepted his destiny. His achievements made him one of the most influential Lithuanians of the XIX century.

The brand new Bishop Valančius swung into action from the first day of his reign. Here the early and tho-

24

rough preparation came in good stead. He knew exactly what the nation needed and went after it.

His first goal was to organize a staff of younger priests to help him, not only to formulate ideas but also to carry out plans of action. A strict and very able administrator, he did not have any problem in organizing just such a group. Later, these men proved to be of invaluable help for the Bishop who sought to change nothing less than the very face of a nation.

Thus prepared, Bishop Valančius tackled the first of his major goals — education of the masses. The action was three-pronged.

First, he turned his energies to the youth. Having convinced himself that only through education can the people achieve better living conditions and, ultimately, freedom, he spared nothing to make education a reality. Every pastor in the diocese was instructed to organize a school and every child to attend it. Furthermore, he instructed all teachers to use the language of the people — mostly Lithuanian. On top of that, the Bishop himself traveled extensively throughout the diocese teaching adults catechism, inspecting schools, organizing libraries. All this activity achieved enthusiastic support from the people themselves. Only four years later, his diocese boasted 197 schools and over 5,000 students. So successful were his endeavors that in some parishes illiteracy was wiped out in a matter of a few years. (In mid-XIX century such a record was remarkable indeed and compared very favorably with that of several countries of Western Europe.)

Together with the drive for mass education, Bishop Valančius turned his attention to alcoholism which was rampant and State supported. (It was no coincidence

Bishop Motiejus Valančius

that liquor was the only commodity in Lithuania which was abundant and very cheap. The Czarist government used liquor as a political tool, and quite successfully, at least for a time.). In his drive to stamp out the sickness, he used various methods, not the least of them temperence brotherhoods. In only a few years a network of these prohibition clubs blanketed his diocese and overflowed in other parts of Lithuania. Success was instant and if not complete, at least eliminated the problem as a critical social illness.

The third prong of his attack was his prolific pen. He began writing while still a young seminarian, and never ceased. While organizing schools, he realized the tragic need for children's books. Soon such books by the thousand reached children in the Lithuanian language. Fighting against alcoholism, he published a series of pamphlets, some of which reached 40,000 in the first printing, an unheard of figure at that time. He did not stop there either. As the years went by, he published book after book of short stories, religious subjects, translations, didactic booklets for children. Among them "Žemaičių Vyskupystė" a highly regarded historical study about his own diocese, several ethnographical studies, etc.

A capable intellectual, Bishop Valančius in most of his writings lowered himself to the level of his readers — the poor, newly literate peasantry. At the same time, he used the purest of Lithuanian, so seldom heard among the educated. In this way, he not only captured vast masses of readers, but also imbued the Lithuanian folk with the love of their officially forbidden language, which at that time together with Catholicism constituted the two elements which kept the nation united. Needless to say, most of his writings had also sociological and political overtones.

All these messages were not lost even on the unsophisticated readers. Neither was the oppressive Russian government fooled. Many times the good Bishop was fined and threatened. At the end of his life, he was slated to be deported to Siberia. Only unprecedented outburst by thousands of his flock prevented the Governor General from carrying out this dastardly act.

As the Czarist government's repression tightened, Bishop Valančius became increasingly more active and defiant. Various punishments followed and so did the good Bishop's everincreasing action.

In this, Bishop Valančius and the masses were aided by several other developments. Unrelated as they were, they nevertheless shaped conditions which in turn served as a springboard for future action.

On the one hand, new and modern ideas were quite common among the Lithuanian youth, which after the old and venerable University of Vilnius was closed in 1832, were scattered throughout Russian universities. The youth, as always, more open-minded, more socially conscious, more politically liberal, were clamoring for new and enlightened policies. Their ideas slowly seeped through the darkness and found a fertile soil in the masses.

On the other hand, not all the aristocracy in Russia as well as in Lithuania were completely satisfied with the existing socio-economic conditions and the political structure. There was a minority (a very small minority to be sure) which entertained progressive ideas. One of those ideas was abolishment of serfdom. True, very little was actually accomplished for many decades, but the idea, especially because it was expounded by the landowners themselves, was beneficial and welcome to the few common leaders in their fight for improvements.

Helpful, if only to a degree, was also a new style and awareness in literature. A hightened interest in folklore, national languages, customs and traditions focused attention to the rich and untapped folklore of Lithuania as well as Lithuanian language and history. This interest had very little to do with political or social action, but it did help in terms of Lithuanian self-respect and self-consciousness.

Last, but not least, even the closed society of Imperial Russia was not immune to the revolutionary influence emanating from the three great revolutions: French, American, and Industrial. Although the alien ideas coming from faraway shores were by no means universally embraced, they nevertheless found some fertile and receptive minds. At the very least, these rumblings in the Western World caused ripples in the giant, super-conservative empire.

These several influences slowly but surely helped to create a revolutionary atmosphere. It heated up especially after the Crimean War of 1853-1855. In Lithuania secret youth organizations came into existence aided and abeted by considerable force of political exiles from the 1831 revolt.

An influx of new ideas was intesified after the 1859 amnesty which precipitated the return of several hundred of these exiles back to Lithuania. Their Western experience, modern outlook and deep hatred intensified the revolutionary fever to the point of quite extensive defiance of the rulers and their policies.

A new revolutionary impetus was added by the Czar himself who finally in 1861 , issued a proclamation abolishing serfdom. (At that time, Russia and its occupied countries were the only ones where serfdom still existed as a legal part of socio-economic structure.)

An historic reform in itself, the abolishment of serf-dom was used by the government also as a political tool. The Czarist regime was primarily motivated not by human or social consideration, but political. Abolishment was to serve two basic goals: pacification of the ever more restless peasantry, and separation of the aristocracy from the masses. In this, the government succeeded, but for a price. (Actually, the alienation between the two segments had much deeper roots and a complete break would have occurred anyway.)

The emancipation of the serfs, although an official act of the Czarist regime concurred in by many Lithuanian landowners, was not intended to be a genuine and speedy process. On the one hand, the corrupt Czarist political structure had no intentions to pursue a genuine social reform. On the other hand, the landowners although in favor of reform, did not envision it as anything more than a token change. Both, however, did not take into account the most important factor — the masses themselves.

The abolishment, naturally, was viewed differently by the serfs. After centuries of deprivation, they were impatient, demanding justice and freedom now. Small defiant disturbances errupted the very same year. The aristocracy balked and petitioned help from the government which gladly complied. This only served to kindle the flame which finally erupted into a full-blown revolt in 1863.[8]

The insurrection first started in Poland. Soon the fighting began in Lithuania. In a few short months, the whole country was embraced in the struggle. However, to no avail. As in 1831, the more powerful government forces within eighteen months crushed the insurrection completely. Hundreds of fighters fell on the battlefield, hundreds more were executed, while thousands were exiled to Siberia. A stream of exiles again swelled the ranks of previous political refugees in Western Europe and the United States.

The Czarist vengence was cruel and fierce. To crush the revolt, the government dispatched General Muravjov (1796-1886), whose infamous previous deeds earned him the title of "The Hangman". He was thorough and merciless and lived up to his gruesome nickname.

Executions and deportations were only a part of his plan. A much larger "pacification" program was conceived and implemented. The aristocracy's self-government was immediately abolished. In its place a military police structure was established, assuring the Russians complete control of the country.

The program had several basic points since General Muravjov wanted not only to pacify the country but to Russianize it completely. To achieve this, he first had to crush the Catholic Church, then the aristocracy, and finally the growing national self-assertiveness.

He achieved neither. Although the battle was lost, the struggle was gaining momentum.

The aristocracy, mostly Polonized as it was, now much more severely punished for the insurrection than other segments of the population, soon lost all interest in political affairs and removed itself from the national struggle. Corrupt and spoiled, now beaten, it concentrated in the economic field, trying to save its riches and privileges.

The Church terrorized, its schools closed, its Bishops and priests harasssed by the secret police, not only did not give in, but mounted a powerful and defiant fight. A large part of the clergy were also Polonized and did not play a role in the national struggle. However, quite a few coupled their fight for religious freedom with the burning desire for national identity. The coupling of these two basic ideals later gave birth to Christian Democracy.

The awakening national consciousness was also not to be crushed. To subdue it, the Czarist regime closed many schools. In the remaining ones, the Lithuanian language was again forbidden. Finally, even all publications in the Lithuanian language in Latin characters were outlawed. This to no avail. The suffering, deprivation, and humiliation gave birth to a national spirit never to be extinguished again.

In terms of progress of Christian Democratic thought, we already mentioned Bishop Valančius, whose personality and actions dominated this period. His was the evolutionary road to Christian Democracy. The revolutionary concept in the genesis of Lithuanian Christian Democracy in this period was represented by now by a large group of priests who participated in the revolt. *Father Antanas Mackevičius* [9] (1828-1863) was maybe one of the most prominent of them. He was a commoner by birth and very popular among them. A born leader he immediately organized sizable groups of guerillas and took personal command. After numerous battles he was badly wounded, captured and finally executed by hanging.

His policies had all the ideas later to flourish in Christian Democratic thought. While the Polonized nobility waged their own battles, Father Mackevičius and his fellow priests — leaders of the peasantry joined the insurrection with the force made-up entirely of peasants and serfs. While the nobility was fighting for their privileges, Father Mackevičius joined the struggle to advance the cause of the common man. Lastly, while the land-

32

Rev. Antanas Mackevičius

owners dreamed about re-establishing the defunct Lithuanian-Polish Commonwealth, Father Mackevičius and his fellow leaders and troops ascertained and proclaimed as their goal, Lithuania's independence not only from Russia, but from Poland as well. As a matter of fact historical studies show that political freedom was an even more important goal than any other.[10]

6

THE BEGINNING OF
THE MOVEMENT

The insurrection of 1863 marks a very definite point in the Lithuanian national re-awakening as well as in the genesis of Lithuanian Christian Democratic thought. Historical analysis and perspective yield several insights.

First, it substantially weakened the economic grip of the estranged nobility upon the peasantry.

Second, it provided a much improved economic basis for the common people which was of major importance for the national struggle. This actually was a welcome by-product of the Czarist policy. As mentioned before, the regime tried to alienate the Lithuanian nobility from the masses. To achieve this, the government, after the revolt, not only speeded up the land reform, but actually liberalized its application to the benefit of the peasantry. This policy was much more restricted and tokenized elsewhere in the Russian empire.

Third, more advantageous economic conditions enabled many more Lithuanian youths of common stock to seek a higher education. Many of these later became national leaders in the struggle for independence.

Fourth, an oppressive policy towards the Catholic Church yielded a crop of new clergy of common birth whose faith, social ideas, and national ideals evolved into a unity of purpose which later gave birth to Lithuanian Christian Democracy.

Fifth, the suppression of everything Lithuanian only stiffened the backbone of the newly emancipated majority of the populous.

Sixth, the nobility's decline as a leading political force created a vacuum of national power which was then seized by the patriotic peasantry through their educated sons, a small but genuinely nationalistically oriented group of leaders.

It is also of note that this period produced the first national leaders who were laymen as opposed to clergymen who for decades were in the forefront of national reawakening.

Thus, under these changed conditions, the beaten but not defeated nation continued to struggle against Russian oppression and for self-identity.

One of the most unusual and important facets of this struggle was the fight for, and with, the printed word. Thanks to Bishop Valančius' efforts, the literacy rate in Lithuania at that time was high. However, the Russians outlawed all printing in Lithuanian in Latin characters.[1] To overcome this literary genocide, Bishop Valančius and others organized an ingenious network of publishing books in East Prussia and smuggling them to Lithuania proper. During the forty years of printing blackout, thousands upon thousands of books were thus printed and distributed by 2,000 book carriers.[2] (East Prussia is a part of ethnographic Lithuania, at that time occupied by the Germans, now incorporated into the Soviet Union.)

Another turnpoint in the struggle came in 1883, when the first Lithuanian newspaper *"Aušra"* (The Dawn)[3] was published in Ragainė (Ragnit), and Tilžė (Tilsit) East Prussia. It was conceived and edited by *Dr. Jonas Basanavičius*,[4] an exiled physician living in Bulgaria, later chairman of the National Council and the Father of Modern Lithuania.

"Aušra" was a non-partisan newspaper and its contribution spanned the whole spectrum of Lithuanian thought. It lasted only three years, but its importance cannot be overemphasized. Its short duration was due to yet another important phenomenon: a natural process of ideological differentiation among the leadership.

As a punishment for the 1831 Revolt, the Russians closed the University of Vilnius in 1832 hoping that the Lithuanian youths would be easier Russianized while attending Russian universities. (For this reason, Lithuanians were also forbidden to attend Western European Schools.) The policy was not particularly successful. However, many of these students were greatly influenced by the religious liberalism which was popular in those universities. In practice, these students became non-practicing Catholics, critical of dogmas and Church authority. Quite a few of them became also followers of Socialism. It was only a matter of time before this religious liberalism and political socialism manifested itself in the public life and print of Lithuania. This differentiation thus was the cause of the closing of *"Aušra"*. It was a price to be paid for newly achieved sophistication. The Catholic leadership, which

37

for decades led the struggle against oppression, which even now was waging a very hard fight for the Church, and which wholeheartedly supported *"Aušra"*, could not and did not accept ideas which were against the very grain of their beliefs.

After several tries to resolve this falling-out on ideological grounds (politically there was always a complete unity between both segments) the Catholic forces in 1889 issued their own newspaper *"Apžvalga"* (The Review).[5] This was the *first Christian Democratic* periodical in Lithuanian. It also marked the birth of the Lithuanian Christian Democratic movement. The ensuing period lasted until 1905 and is characterized by *political and social education action.*

"Apžvalga" was printed in East Prussia, as were all Lithuanian books and periodicals at that time. The newspaper as well as the movement did not have as yet a program or defined political aims. It did, however, have a clear overall goal which was formulated as "a fight for religious and national freedom". The editors never doubted that the Russian empire would one day collapse and all enslaved nations would be free. *"Apžvalga"* thus, unequivocally, time and time again declared that it was fighting for "Lithuanian Motherland".

Even at this early stage in the movement, *"Apžvalga"* was explicit in its principle beliefs: *Christianity, Democracy, and Lithuanianism.* In one of its editorials the newspaper said: "Our guideline is — Catholicism and Lithuanianism. From these guidelines we will never waiver, come hell or high water, even if we have to sacrifice our very lives for it." [6] Democracy was also stressed, basically in terms of better living conditions and equal human rights for all people, especially for the disadvantaged.

38

The newspaper's influence was immeasurable. It was a fighting periodical which gave not quarter to anybody who was against its goals. Issue after issue it pounded the Czarist regime with ever-increasing tenacity. It did not believe in any compromise or letup. Its road was ramrod straight and the editors never waivered. Therein lied its greatest accomplishment. Taking into consideration the prevailing conditions and the spirit of the time "Apžvalga" served its purposes extremely well. Subjugated, suffering and humiliated nation needed encouragement and "Apžvalga" gave it abundantly. It formed the right public opinion which was in line with the general feeling of the people. It expressed the feelings of an occupied country in no uncertain way.

"Apžvalga" was edited by an unusual and dedicated man, *Father Kazimieras Pakalniškis* (1866-1933).[7] Unusual only in a sense that he was one of the most successful Russian baiter of his time. Himself of common birth, he like his predecessors, from his very youth joined in the struggle for the masses and against the oppressors. Of modest literary talent, he nevertheless achieved a highly respectful status among the period's writers. His dedication was single-minded, and his commentaries on the Russian occupation devastatingly accurate. Even more important than political commentary was his short-short stories which the unsophisticated serfs read and re-read with great delight. His fighting spirit and stubborness was needed, but to a degree, these qualities were also the downfall of the paper.

The newspaper's demise came six years later when in 1896 another Christian Democratic newspaper was organized. Historians propose several reasons for its demise as well as for the birth of *"Tėvynės Sargas"* (The Guardian

39

of Homeland). It seems that *"Apžvalga"* was considered by some to be too harsh on liberals and their ideas, too coarse in its polemics with them, too uncompromising with the Polonized clergy (still in the majority), etc. Be as it may, the new periodical more than amply served Christian Democratic needs as well as the aspirations of the Catholic population. (The liberal ideas and thoughts of the time were expounded by another periodical — *"Varpas"* (The Bell), which also played a most significant role in the course of Lithuanian national re-awakening. Both periodicals are still published today: *"Tėvynės Sargas"* by the Christian Democrats and *"Varpas"* by the Populists).

"Tėvynės Sargas"[8] was organized by young patriotic Catholic clergy who also financed its publication. It was edited by several editors of whom *Canon Juozas Tumas-Vaižgantas*[9] (1869-1933) was the most prominent. The late great leader of the Lithuanian Christian Democrats, Dr. Kazys Pakštas saw Canon Tumas-Vaižgantas as "A synthesis of Lithuanian patriotism, Christian humanism, profound democracy and cultural idealism".[10] Novelist *Antanas Vaičiulaitis* describes him as "One of the most popular personalities in all Lithuania. His name was spoken even in the lowliest cottage of the most distant village. Everyone was eager to catch a glimpse of him. He was "of a lively disposition," was "an irrepressible optimist," was "always available for public service," and was "ever ready to do a favor." "Editor, devout priest, crusader in Lithuanianism from his earliest days, publicist, silver-tongued orator, university professor, and a writer with twenty volumes to his credit — such was Vaižgantas, a man of noble and magnanimous heart".[11]

40

Canon Juozas Tumas-Vaižgantas

Later, the same Canon Vaižgantas will play a significant role in organizing Christian Democrats, and even a more significant role as one of the greatest Lithuanians of his time.

"*Tėvynės Sargas'* " motto was "Love God more than anything, your neighbor as yourself, and your Homeland more than self". Nationality was closely aligned with religion, although, the latter was given priority. This coupling of nationality and Catholicism had a very distinct purpose — to stop Polonization of the masses through the mostly Polonized Lithuanian clergy. It succeeded admirably.

The newspaper took particular interest in achieving the abolishment of printing restrictions in Lithuanian. Almost every issue (from 32 to 60 pages) carried accounts of the persecution by the Russian gendarmes, ways and means of fighting for the printing rights, forms of petitions to be delivered to the Governor and the Czar himself requesting freedom of expression, etc. It also consistently condemned the restrictions put on the Lithuanian language in primary and secondary schools, courts of law and public offices. It incessantly fought against the Orthodox Church's privileges in religious matters, for religious freedom in general and, for the right to practice professions in Lithuania.

The periodical was also adamant in demanding freedom and liberty. However, in this matter, it took a more gradualistic approach to the problem, especially in comparison with "*Apžvalga*", although it otherwise followed in its predecessor's footsteps. The difference was really more of form than principle.

Two more subjects were of particular interest to "*Tėvynės Sargas*". One was education and, the other, economic well-being. It was persistent in its reprimands to the Polonized or the Russianized nobility and clergy, openly propagated boycotting of Russian schools, etc.

Just as persistently, the editors proclaimed the beneficial effects of saving, thriftness, economic freedom, the tragedies of poverty, litigations, etc.

It was also more tolerant and did not hesitate to acknowledge points made by rival papers. It did indulge in polemic with the positivist *"Varpas"*,[12] but on a higher plane than its predecessor.

As far as the Christian Democratic movement is concerned, *"Tėvynės Sargas"* acted as a catalyst for the scattered activists. However, even the newspaper, as a rallying point, did not cause organization and consolidation. The movement did not have either a formal program or popularly elected leadership. There were no chapters or conferences. To a degree, this lack of organization was purposely maintained because of the prevailing conditions. The more prominent activists also felt that program and organization might create a bureaucratic network, which would only hinder the dissemination of ideas throughout the country.

The next few years, however, brought substantial changes all around. The Russo-Japanese War ended with a Russian fiasco. That triggered the more modern intelligencia to openly revolt against the corrupt Czarist regime. Demands for a constitution, for personal liberty, and for freedom of the press echoed throughout the empire.

The enslaved nations did not waste a second to join in the general turmoil with their own specific demands. In Lithuania, this revolutionary movement concentrated itself first on freedom of the press which for forty years had

43

been denied. The shaken Czarist regime gave in and, in 1904, the fight was won. More than that — tight reign on cultural life was also relaxed.

As the fever increased, the whole country began to organize. Among demands for more cultural, educational and press freedom, here and there Lithuanians raised the question of political freedom and national independence.

Thus, new situations demanded new approaches. The Socialists already organized several years before; had their leadership and a formal program. The Christian Democratic movement, however, was even worse off than before. *"Tėvynės Sargas"* ceased publishing several years prior and, thus, the only rallying point was no more. No one really represented in an organized way the Catholic point of view: the older clergy, as was stated before, had in many cases little to do with the Lithuanian re-awakening, and the younger, patriotic priests with the other Christian inspired laymen, were still unorganized. The situation called for action.

THE ADOPTION OF THE
FIRST FORMAL PROGRAM

As mentioned in the previous chapter, the situation
in the wake of the Crimean debackle was pregnant with
revolutionary fervor, grandiose expectations and overflow-
ing energy. In Lithuania, as in other enslaved countries,
this was a time of bee-like activity. The opportunity was
too good to be passed by without exhausting all available
ways and means to improve the nation's lot.

The Christian Democratic movement, about this time,
was growing out of its "childhood" and entering "young
adulthood".[1] Its scattered activists needed guidance, its
ideas a new concise expression. This new impetus came
first from St. Petersburg and later from Vilnius.

St. Petersburg, at that time, boasted the only Catholic
Theological Academy. It was organized by Lithuanians in
Vilnius in 1834. Later (in 1842), the Czarist government
transferred it to St. Petersburg, so it would be able to

better keep an eye on it. In 1867, it was forcibly merged with the only other theological academy, that of Warsaw. Thus, for many years, it was the only postgraduate school in Catholic theology in the whole Russian empire. From the very beginning, Lithuanian theologians played prominent roles in the academy. In 1904, among the faculty, there were three young Lithuanians: *Pranas Būčys*, (age 32), *Jonas Maironis-Mačiulis* (age 42), and *Aleksandras Jakštas-Dambrauskas* (age 44). They took upon themselves the task of preparing the first written Christian Democratic Program. They called it *"A Draft of the Program of the Lithuanian Christian Democratic Alliance"*. It was a document of great consequence in general and, even more important, one for Christian Democracy in particular. For this reason, the following lengthly excerpts are provided. It should be stressed that it is an expression of Christian Democratic thought of 70 years ago by people who were occupied and exploited. Only in this framework the deep meaning and beauty of the document can be fully appreciated.[2]

The draft is divided into eight chapters and subdivided into over fifty paragraphs. In the preamble titled "The Alliance of Lithuanian Christian Democrats", the learned authors first, carefully spell out the meaning of a political party. The succeeding paragraphs are concerned directly with Christian Democracy.

"We, Lithuanian Christian Democrats, have also joined together because our thoughts about Lithuania's affairs are also very similar among us. In our alliance we are Lithuanians, all are Christians, and all are democrats. The very word 'democracy' was not known in Lithuania until very recently: thus, many people to this day are ignorant of its meaning."

"Democrats are all those people, who first of all and mostly, concern themselves with the plight of the common people. The democrats are striving to achieve a society in which the poor people, just as the rich people, would have the same political rights, the same privileges to vote for any representatives to the parliament. We, who belong to this Lithuanian Christian Democratic Alliance, will do everything possible that the common people of Lithuania would be guaranteed their right to everything good and decent. We will try to ease their life. We will see that the cities will not exploit the farmer, his family and his earnings. We will see that they will not hurt his soul and his health. We will work to ease the burden of those who live in villages; peasants who have or do not have land; those who hire labor and laborers; sharecroppers and farmhands. We will aid those, who migrate to cities looking for a better life, and stay there."

"We call ourselves Christians and use this word in our organizational title because we believe that there is a God and that Christ is our Redeemer. We accept the teachings of Jesus and His laws we shall obey. We will follow the Christian precepts not only within the boundaries of our households, but also within the framework of our national policies. In this faithful adherence to God and religion, we demonstrate our difference from the other two parties in Lithuania. The Social Democrats do not believe in religion, and the Lithuanian Democrats neither talk about religion nor care for it. Knowing that religion is most vital to everyone, we will defend it everywhere and everytime."

"We purposely entered the Lithuanian name into our organizational title. This is because Lithuania is our fatherland and we love her just as children love their mother.

Bishop Pranciškus Būčys

"The Lithuanian language is dearest to us above all languages. However, we will never show intolerance to others who speak other tongues in Lithuania or anyplace, because we are Christians and as such, we love our neighbors. Every nationality has its own language. We are Lithuanians and our language is Lithuanian."

"The cause of today's misfortunes is the lack of human conscience. The bureaucrats tortured and cheated us because they did not have a conscience. Thus, if those who dedicate themselves to fight bureaucracy, and will at the same time forget their conscience, one group of usurpers will be replaced by another group of like usurpers. Realizing this, we pledge never to engage in a fight with our foes using unethical means and methods. We will never execute our enemies, we will not plunder their riches, we will not accuse them falsely, because such behaviour is unethical and demeaning. We begin with God and with God we shall also work towards our goals."

"Our Alliance embraces the large majority of the Lithuanian clergy. We have the blessings of our Bishops."

The first chapter is entitled "General Goals of the Program of Lithuanian Christian Democrats". Excerpts follow:

"Lithuania must be granted autonomy, with her own parliament, which shall be elected by secret ballot, under universal franchise by direct and equal methods. Lithuanian autonomy shall mean all ethnographic boundaries. As members of the eventual Russian parliament, Lithuanian Christian Democrats will always strive for morality, justice and freedom. The Alliance will always fight against religious persecution and restrictions. We will also strive for political unity with all other Lithuanian parties in all matters concerning Lithuania. In the basic law of Russia, there shall be written, that the government shall be constitutional; that the ministers of state shall be responsible to the representatives of the people; that the state finances shall be controlled by the representatives of the people; that all nations residing within the borders of Russia shall have the right to autonomy; and, that all people shall be equal before the courts of justice", etc. The list is long. The document also demands freedom of speech, religion, press, and gatherings.. It stresses the absolute necessity of an educational system responsible to the people and responsive to their wishes and needs. Finally, it demands equal political rights for women.

The second chapter, called "General Matters Concerning Lithuania" is just as demanding.

"The goal of Lithuanian Christian Democratic action is full autonomy for Lithuania in its ethnographic boundaries, i. e. the region of Kaunas, all those parts of Suvalkai, Kuršai and Gardinas regions where Lithuanians are predominant, and all of the region of Vilnius with the City of Vilnius, which is the capital of the country. The autonomy shall mean these national rights: to have a parliament in Vilnius, empowered to legislate and levy taxes, elected by the people; to have the other two branches of government — executive and judicial, consisting of local people; to have all schools teaching in Lithuanian by Lithuanians; the executive to be responsible to local parliament", etc.

The third chapter, concerns itself with the educational system. "At the very outset, and with the greatest emphasis, we demand that all subjects at the grade school level be taught in Lithuanian; that all teachers be Lithuanians; that the curriculum be responsive to the needs and wishes of local population; that high schools have special classes in Lithuanian; that religion be taught by a priest of the same religion as the pupils; that Lithuanian language classes in the teachers colleges be made one of the most important subjects", etc.

The fourth chapter deals exclusively with the Lithuanian language. "We will take all necessary measures that Polonization and Russification be stopped immediately. There must be a Lithuanian priest in every parish to which at least 300 Lithuanian speaking people belong. If the number reaches 1000, the sermons and other devotional services must be conducted in Lithuanian. In any diocese boasting 100,000 Lithuanian Catholics, the ordinary or at least one auxiliary bishop must be a Lithuanian." The chapter further states that all officials in Lithuania must speak Lithuanian and conduct the public business in Lithuanian.

Chapter five deals with economic and social matters. Several important points are covered. Among them: distribution of state-owned lands to peasants without land who want to become farmers; organization of public welfare apparatus; organization of credit unions; establishment of hospitals and nursing homes, especially for the poor, at public expense; and, organization of sick benefits and social security system, again, primarily for the poor.

Ethical and moral points are covered in chapter six. Here, Christian Democrats demand adequate protection for working women; promise to organize special task forces to help women; and fight against alcoholism, and outline their own program in those two fields.

Chapter seven is called "Church Matters". The main points: "Free communication with the Holy Father. Bishops are to be appointed according to Cannon Law. Diocesan government is to be administered by the Church

51

Msgr. Jonas Mačiulis-Maironis

without any outside interference whatsoever. The **Bishops** must be free to establish new parishes and re-organize the existing ones, as well as, call diocesan synods and build churches, chapels, etc. Also, all lands and other wealth nationalized by the government must be returned to the lawful owner, the Catholic Church." Finally, the document demands the return of the Theological Academy back to Vilnius. However, the most important and truly modern statement, in the last paragraph, unequivocally states freedom for all religions.

The concluding chapter (the eighth) outlines the party organization and its governing body. The main points: "The Central Committee of the Lithuanian Christian Democrats is to be elected by county delegates prior to each annual party congress and consist of five members. The Central Committee resides in Vilnius". The lengthy chapter further on details the party organization down to the parish and county level, enumerates the duties and responsibilities of every elected party official, lists the particular fields of endeavor in which the party should be especially active, etc.

Without even attempting a lengthly and in-depth analysis of this first program, several points must be made in order to highlight the significance of this document.

As was mentioned before, it must be borne in mind that these theses were expounded more than seventy years ago, at the time when democracy in Europe, as we understand it today, was in its infancy. It is even more remarkable, because these precepts were born in a nation which was, at the time, in the throws of severe subjugation by an ultraconservative and militaristic power for more than a century. This historic perspective is of utmost relevance to the analysis of the program.

In general, the most astounding fact about the program is its modern approach to social and political problems. Very few documents of that time are as explicit in their pure democratic thought as this program. It is a declaration of democratic principles far ahead of its time.[3]

This is amply illustrated by several statements. We already mentioned the great emphasis on democratic precepts, institutions and processes. No less important and interesting are the social and economic aspects of this program. Social security, land reform, health insurance and similar ideas were surely ahead of their time even within today's framework. So are the purely governmental declarations: the principles of representative government, the separation of the several branches of the government, universal franchise, etc. (Even equal rights for women, an idea which to this day is not universally accepted.)

On the other hand, several ideas of the document sound at least controversial, although this controversiality is actually superficial.

First, the stout defense of Catholicism does sound rather strange in the same context with the similarly strong defense of liberal democratic thought and process. However, this affirmative and seemingly exclusive posture towards Catholism was actually defensive in nature. It must be remembered that the Greek Orthodox faith and the Church of Russia at that time was not only the privileged religious body in the country, but it let itself to be used by the government as a political tool. Thus, the defense of Catholicism was not only a defense against unwanted missionary zeal of an alien faith, but also in a more general way, a statement of the nation's determination to chart its own independent course politically.

Second, the seemingly overstated case of Lithuanian nationalism is also easily explained. As outlined in previous chapters, Lithuanianism under the Russian occupation was in an extremely precarious position. The Czarist government spared no efforts to Russianize the whole population, while the Polonized Lithuanian nobility was similarly introducing alien cultural ideas to the country. Thus, it is understandable that to keep their national identity, Lithuanians had to have strong national goals before them. (This was typical to all three political movements. Social Democrats and Lithuanian Democrats were just as firm and explicit in their programs on this subject.)

Finally, who were the three young priests whose great intellect and remarkable political maturity gave birth to this extraordinary document.

Canon Jonas Maciulevičius-Maironis (1862-1932), later monsignor, theologian, professor and rector of priest seminary is now known as one of the greatest Lithuanian poets of all times. A prolific writer he was indeed a prophet in his many books of poetry. Novelist Antanas Vaičiulaitis (himself a writer of great talent) in his *"Outline History of Lithuanian Literature"* (Chicago, 1942) says this about Maironis: "With his unmatched verses, he roused the nation by speaking of Lithuania's natural beauty, recalling the great and ancient past, drawing word pictures of historic castles and recounting the glorious deeds of the ancestors of Lithuanians. He inspired all with the love of their country, its language, and its people. His poetic talent was so great, and his wings of inspiration carried him over such wide expanse, that he was able to avoid all didactism; the poet became identical with his ideal; he and his people whom he was leading were a

Msgr. Aleksandras Dambrauskas-Jakštas

single entity. Maironis was not only one of the most distinguished fashioners of poetic language and verse form, but he was also unreservedly the most popular poet. His clear euphonious speech, sincerity of feeling, and easily comprehensible ideas drew him close to everyone. Even today, his songs are heard in every knook and corner of Lithuania. With the new invasion, Maironis' poetry became even more real; to the Lithuanian people, burdened with brutal oppression, his words were a source of spiritual strength, a battle cry, a promise of ultimate victory."

Very little can be added to the last sentences, except that it is as true today as it was 32 years ago: Maironis' poems are recited to this day by every Lithuanian the world over; his songs are echoing at every occasion, his hymns are sung in churches, in every parish where Lithuanians gather to worship.[4]

Father Aleksandras Dambrauskas-Adomas Jakštas (1860- 1938) later monsignor, was a man of many talents: journalist, theologian, philosopher, mathematician, editor, book publisher, literary critic. His first writings appeared in *"Aušra"* when he was only 24 years old. From then on, he never stopped. He edited dozens of periodicals, and thousands of his articles and essays are scattered in the most prestigious publications. He is also an author of several prayer books, short stories, etc. As a mathematician, he is mostly respected for his work on the new trigonometrical systems and even more for his Lithuanian mathematical terminology. His philosophical and theological ideas are scattered in numerous short essays and three books: *"Science and Religion"*, *"The Problems of Evil"*, and *"The Highest Virtue"*. However, his lasting fame is his critical writings. Very few literary pieces got by him, and for many years he was the only professional critic systematically reviewing the whole spectrum of Lithuanian literature. Literary historians are far from unanimous in their judgments of Jakštas' critical writings although everyone generally concedes that his efforts were at the time invaluable to the overall progress of Lithuanian letters. His encyclopedic mind and makeup scattered his energies over wide fields of endeavor, but every work he ever undertook always had the overtones of Lithuanianism. For this, he was exiled by the Czarist government to the far corner of Russia. For this he was also revered by a grateful nation. For many years he was the most prominent Catholic scholar in Lithuania and the first to be accorded the high title of Academician by the Lithuanian Catholic Science Academy. To this day, he is revered as one of the great Lithuanian patriots, scholars, and writers.[5]

Father Pranciškus Būčys (1872-1951),[6] later Bishop and President of the Lithuanian University of Kaunas, is best known for his pastoral work. In his early priesthood, he chose the monastic life, joined the Marian Fathers Congregation (not to be confused with another congregation of the same name) and was one of the few who resurrected the dying Order. (The Czarist regime was particularly harsh on this religious body and succeeded in decimating it.) Most of his long life was spent in serving his congregation in high offices — twice as Superior General. For many years he also served the Church as the Vatican's special emissary to the Free World's Russian population mostly in missionary endeavors. For this reason, he traveled extensively throughout the world. All along he managed to publish voluminous works mostly on religious subjects. His extensive memoirs have recently been edited and published. Of the three authors, his was the job to introduce the program to the Grand Congress of Vilnius, of which he was one of the presiding officers.[7]

PART III

INDEPENDENCE:
A CHALLENGE

8

THE BIRTH OF THE PARTY

The second impetus for action and organization came in the aftermath of the Grand Congress of Vilnius in 1905.[1]

The idea for the Congress grew out of the general upheaval in Russia and Poland of the same year where it grew to almost revolutionary proportions. In Lithuania, it took a more subdued form characterized mostly by immense cultural activity: proliferation of press, concerts, musical and art life, etc. Political activity was mostly discernable in the Socialist camp, although other political groups were also active. All this activity, very salutary in itself, helped to dramatize one of the shortcomings of the whole Lithuanian movement: that of lack of national political consolidation. Various leaders came to realize that activity and movement must have coordination and direction. This realization gave birth to the idea of a grand congress of all Lithuanians. To organize such a gathering a committee was established headed by Dr. Jonas Basanavičius, revered non-partisan leader of the Lithuanian re-awakening movement. As the first task, the committee published a declaration inviting the representatives of all Lithuania to the Congress. The response was overwhelming. Not only the idea of such a gathering was universally approved, but everyone in the country immediately started the process of electing delegates to this Grand Congress of Vilnius, as the meeting later came to be called.

The Congress convened on November 20, 1905 in the Town Hall of Vilnius. Over 2000 participants took part, representing not only every organization, political party, town, parish, and village, but also Lithuanian exiles in various cities of Russia, Ukraine, Poland, Latvia and other countries as well.[2]

True to the temper of the time, the meeting was stormy and at times explosive.[3] Conceived as a unity conference, the gathering soon became a hotly political conclave dominated by political factions. However, all the commotion notwithstanding, unity did prevail and was most clearly demonstrated in the several general resolutions adopted at the conclusion of the Congress. The resolutions were highlighted by four main points: 1. The Congress unanimously declared the government of Czarist Russia to be the worst enemy of Lithuania; 2. Demanded political autonomy for the country; 3. Outlined ways and means to achieve autonomy; and, 4. Declared that in the country, Lithuanian national interests, as represented by Lithuanian language in schools, churches and public offices must be granted first priority.[4] The very same night that those resolutions were passed, 36,000 copies were printed and distributed throughout the width and breadth of the nation. It had the effect of a wildfire. In countless communities, hundreds of Russian officials, overseers, and teachers were dismissed and replaced by local people; citizens stopped paying taxes; Russian supported liquor stores closed. Here and there, para-military groups were organized, etc.

For a short while, the Russian government acted as if stunned by the happening and did nothing.[5] However, soon repressive measures replaced inaction, as the whole might of the occupying power descended upon the country. Thousands of patriots were exiled to Siberia, as well as imprisoned. Many escaped persecution by emigrating to the Western World, mostly the United States. All reforms, so promising and progressive, were nullified. Only in the educational field, the government allowed certain changes to remain in effect.

All this notwithstanding, the Grand Congress of Vilnius had the most far-reaching consequences in the nation's struggle for freedom.[6] No less important was it for the Christian Democratic Movement.

Christian Democrats attended the Congress in various capacities and in impressive numbers, but as yet, unorganized, without national leadership or a firmly established program. The other two national parties were organized and quite active politically.[7] As a matter of fact, at the beginning of the Congress, both were quite adamant towards the Catholic group, the clergy in particular.[8] Their fighting mood was one of the reasons for Christian Democrats to consolidate rather early in the proceedings and take part as a group. Father Būčys (one of the authors of the first Christian Democratic Program) was elected to the ruling body of the Congress as one of the co-chairman and played a key role in representing the Christian Democratic point of view. Also a very active participant of the Congress was Father Tumas-Vaižgantas, the former editor of *"Tėvynės Sargas"* and by now a prominent Catholic writer and patriot. Several other Christian Democrats were also active, especially after the leftist group proceeded to ignore the Christian Democrats and attempted to rule the deliberations and proceedings. However, a healthy balance was struck after Christian Democrats realized their strength and exercised their considerable power.

This political infighting, even if it did not affect the national unity, left a lasting impression on the Christian Democrats. It proved to them the necessity of good organization and concerted action. Even during the Congress, the brand new program was distributed to the Christian Democratic delegates, and at a caucus, a decision was reached to organize a Central Committee which would immediately take steps to consolidate the movement into a viable and effective political apparatus. Actually, it took several more years before Christian Democrats evolved into a full-fledged political party. There were several reasons for this reluctance. The obvious one was the prevailing political conditions. The country was still occupied by a foreign power which did not hesitate to use any and all means to stamp out insubordination. The other reason was less obvious but similarly important. That was the opposition of the hierarchy and many of the older clergy. As stated elsewhere, both of these most influential segments of the Church were mostly under Polish influence and were alienated from the Lithuanian movement. They also had their own political ideas as well as budding political organizations. It could not be expected that they would readily approve a movement which was not only openly progressive but at the same time, openly and strongly Lithuanian motivated. The analysis proved to be right: the hierarchy did not approve the program. (Although it did not condemn it either.). Under such conditions, the movement's leadership was hesitant openly to defy the hierarchy. Another avenue was clearly indicated and soon found.

Two basic approaches were utilized. One was actual social action on a wide scale. Various Christian Democratic groups organized welfare organizations, established nursing homes for the aged and the afflicted, etc. Other groups were active in organizing the sharecroppers and farm hands; defended their rights, tried to improve their working conditions; and increase their wages. An outstanding example of the first was a nursing home in Panevėžys, which soon had 200 people under its care.[9] To overcome the shortage of specialists, several nuns were imported from Austria to administer the home. An example of the latter was Father Tumas-Vaižgantas' activities in his parish. He was the first one to organize a large Christian Democratic Chapter in Vadatkai (December 7, 1905) which became very active and creative especially in terms of social action.[10] At the very first meeting, the Vadatkai Chapter proposed an array of demands: complete freedom of religion, political autonomy within ethnographic borders, use of Lithuanian language in schools, public offices, and churches, effective agrarian reform, local self-government, abolishment of police bureaucracy, improvement of working conditions in large estates, improved communications, transportation, and so on.

Father Tumas-Vaižgantas and his Christian Democrats were one of the first who not only tried to live up to their own established program, but succeeded at it. Only six days later, Father Tumas-Vaižgantas called a meeting of the regions' estateholders, members of his chapter and farm laborers, at which a labor contract of sorts was hammered out. True, it bears little resemblance to today's labor contracts, however, seventy years ago, it was an unheard of labor document, thoroughly progressive and radical. In it the Christian Democrats induced the employers to agree to the following conditions: night work was to be abolished; every sick farm laborer received two months sick pay if on sick status; if illness continued, half pay for the next two months; the estateholder was responsible for medical and medicinal costs incurred by the laborer or a member of his family; the farm laborer's wife would not have to work, but, if she wished to do so, she must be paid as any other laborer; all disagreements would be arbitrated by a joint committee consisting of employers, employees and the local priest; estateholders who were a party to this agreement, and who would not abide by it, would be boycotted completely. Many more paragraphs of this agreement dealt with significant details.[11] It was a victory for which Christian Democracy gained in popularity, although it also brought sorrow to its author. For a while, the landowners honored the agreement and the Russian overseers did not react. But not for very long. Only a few years later, both the estateholders and the Polonized clergy mounted a smear campaign against Father Tumas-Vaižgantas which played right into the hands of the occupying power. To escape imprisonment, he went into temporary hiding. Without him the Christian Democratic chapter folded. However, the seeds had been planted.

Similar activities were taking place throughout the country. Chapter after chapter sprung into being and social action. In most cases, along with social improvement, purely political action also followed based upon achieving national independence.

The second approach was educational and ideological in nature. This was accomplished in two ways: by meetings and lectures, and by special publications together with numerous articles in the Catholic press. On the one hand, younger priests who embraced Christian Democracy devoted many a sermon on social aspects of Catholicism and the teachings of the Church. In this connection two encyclicals (Pope Leo XIII's *Rerum Novarum* and *Graves de Communi*) played an immense role. Sociology courses began to appear in priest seminaries taught by professors whose humble birth and Western European schooling made them especially effective bearers of Christian Democratic precepts. Clergy conferences more and more concerned themselves with the lot of the underprivileged, the laborers, farmhands, and socio-economic problems in general. Of extraordinary importance was a Social Problems Conference at Kaunas at which *Father Matulaitis* (later Archbishop of Vilnius and now a candidate for sainthood) presented a classic argument for a long overdue land reform and its moral justification. (Later this very same saintly man played one of the key roles when the Land Reform Law was debated in Christian Democratic circles and the Lithuanian Diet itself.)

On the other hand, Christian Democratic ideas found their way to the masses through the press. In 1906 a new Christian Democratic magazine "Šaltinis" (The Fountainhead) appeared. Two years later it was joined by another — "*Vadovas*" (The Leader) which, although not a Christian Democratic paper, devoted ample space to Christian Democratic writings. Available to Christian Democrats was yet another journal *"Draugija"* (The Society) a prestigious scholarly publication, edited by one of the authors of the first Christian Democratic program.[12] As a matter of fact, *"Draugija"* was the first one to publish the program in its entirety.[13] Along with these periodicals, a series of pamphlets, booklets and scholarly papers were published and soon gained wide circulation. Already in 1905, a booklet was published in Panevėžys by the name of "Christian Democracy". Two years later, *Father Kazimieras Šaulys* (later one of the signers of the Declaration of Independence and a high official of the Archdiocese of Kaunas) authored a booklet on *"The Socialists and Social Questions"* in which he also expounded on Christian Democracy. That same year Father Šaulys published in *"Draugija"* a highly regarded paper on *"Democracy and Christian Democrats in Terms of the Encyclicals Based on Christian Sociology"*. With every year, the number of publications increased and steadily gained wider acceptance.

9

TOWARDS INDEPENDENCE

By the time World War I started, Lithuanian Christian Democrats were a political power throughout the land. Lithuanian movement in general was also getting stronger by the day.

The war brought mixed blessings for both — Lithuania and the Christian Democrats. At the beginning of the war, a conference was held in Vilnius at which two important decisions were made. First, a new program, adapted to anticipated conditions, was adopted. Second, the as yet informal leadership decided among themselves who should endeavor to stay in Lithuania at all costs if and when the Germans drove the Russians out, so as to prevent the country from being without any leadership.[1]

The political analysis evolved in the conference was born out by near future events. The German might soon indeed occupied Lithuania. Thousands of Lithuanians were forcibly exiled to Russia by the retreating Russian military. There, they joined other thousands of their countrymen who voluntarily or forcibly had settled in Russia earlier. (Large colonies of Lithuanian refugees existed in St. Petersburg, Moscow, Voronezh, Ekaterinoslav, Tifliss, even Siberia, Caucasus region, also in Minsk, Charkov, etc.). Until 1917, very little political action was possible. All energies were devoted to help refugees to survive the rigorous war years both in physical and spiritual terms. Conditions temporarily improved during and shortly after the Russian revolution and by then the Christian Democrats were ready for action. Christian Democratic chapters sprung up in every refugee colony, a newspaper, "Vadas" (The Leader) was published, foundations and other special organizations were created to serve the refugees. This was the period when the *first* Central Committee of the Lithuanian Christian Democratic Party was finally established.[2] The first chairman was *Father J. Vailokaitis* (later renowned financial authority). However, this committee lasted but a very short time. Its residence — St. Petersburg did not provide even the minimal conditions for work. The political situation was deteriorating daily.

The second Central Committee was established in Voronezh chaired by Father Mykolas Krupavičius, the greatest Christian Democratic leader of Lithuania. The members of this Committee, after experiencing harrowing days in revolutionary Russia returned to Lithuania in 1918.

Lithuanian acitvity in Russia culminated in Lithuanian Seimas (or Congress) in St. Petersburg on May 27th-June 3, 1917.[3] This gathering was precipitated by the

Rev. Juozas Vailokaitis

events in Russia. Just two months before, the Russian Socialists organized demonstrations which culminated in the
abdication of Czar Nicholas II on March 15, 1917. The
head of the provisional government, Prince Lvov, declared self-determination to the nations of Russia. Lithuanian leaders immediately requested self-rule in those parts
of the country which were not at that time under the
German occupation. The request was not acted upon and
the Lithuanian leadership decided to call a congress to
strengthen its position. The 336 member gathering unanimously declared that "Since Lithuania, until the end of
the XVIII century, had its own separate political life... it
is therefore clearly declared to the whole world: the whole
ethnic Lithuania must become an independent state ... its
government and structure to be determined by a founding Seimas (Diet, Congress, Parliament), elected by universal, equal and secret ballot".[4]

In the deliberations of this Congress, Christian Democrats, led by Father Mykolas Krupavičius and Father J.
Vailokaitis played an increasingly important role. The 39
member delegation was already well organized and politically well versed. After the Congress, the delegation met
with other Christian Democrats and, as mentioned before,
consolidated the party program as well as elected the first
Central Committee.

Meanwhile, most of Lithuania was ruled by the
Germans, who had their own devious designs concerning Lithuania and the other occupied countries. Trying
to outwit the population, they proposed an advisory council which ostensibly would be representative of the people's will. Several national groups fell for it but, not
Lithuanians. They demanded free elections and a natio-

71

nal meeting. The elections, of course, were disallowed, but the Germans consented to the meeting.

The Conference of Vilnius was held September 18-22, 1917, with 214 delegates in attendance.[5] Christian Democrats were well represented and again played an important role. (By this time, the Christian Democrats who stayed in Lithuania were on the verge of being organized, after spending the war years under the German yoke in very energetic political, economic and social activity.) The gathering, which was aware of the resolutions passed by the St. Petersburg Congress, as well as the energetic activities of Lithuanians in the United States, reiterated that "An independent Lithuania must be established within its ethnographic boundaries and based on democratic principles".[6] It also elected a twenty member State Council of Lithuania which later proclaimed the nation's independence. Out of the twenty members, six were Christian Democrats: *A. Stulginskis, Pr. Dovydaitis, K. Bizauskas, J. Vailokaitis, K. Šaulys, and J. Staugaitis, (Actually, eight* Christian Democrats were elected, however, when the socialists objected to too many priests in the Council — six altogether, two of them, both Christian Democrats, voluntarily resigned and were replaced by members of different political parties).[7] Later, on several occasions, the Council changed its membership, eventually expanded to include delegates from Lithuania Minor and other representatives. In the aftermath, a few more Christian Democrats gained membership. (This only showed the great trust that the Christian Democrats commanded in the nation, as well as Christian Democratic political maturity in times of crises.)

Following the conference, the Christian Democrats gathered in caucus (September 23, 1917) and just like

72

their brethren in Russia, a few months later, voted on a new party program and elected a Central Committee with A. *Stulginskis* as Chairman (later, the first constitutionally elected President of the Republic).[8]

Only a few months later, most of the "Russian" Central Committee returned to Lithuanian soil. From the very beginning, it was clear that two parties and two headquarters would be redundant. By that time, the State Council of Lithuania had issued the Proclamation of Independence, the war was at the end, the Russian turmoil was at its peak, the Germans were crushed and the whole world was on a new course. The very same conditions prevailed in Lithuania. The Council valiantly strove to organize the country against enemies from within and without, and to establish order out of all the chaos. Political life was lively and maybe too energetic. No political party could afford the luxury of quiet and prolonged deliberations.

Thus, on November 20, 1918 all Christian Democrats convened in a conference to put their own house in order. (This was the first conference held on independent Lithuanian soil.) Several key problems dominated the meeting. As was mentioned previously, both groups had their own programs. In principle, they were quite alike, however, there were wide gaps in terms of strategy and tactics. One such problem was the question of land reform. Every Christian Democrat, as almost every other member of any political party, was in favor of some such agrarian reform. The question was — how extensive, what type and when? The Vilnius group, with its chairman, A. Stulginskis, cautioned against rash action. The returnees from Russia headed by Father Mykolas Krupavičius, stood foursquare for a radical reform immediately, that is, as soon as

73

conditions permitted. An impasse developed when factions stood firmly by their programs, to be broken only when the conference decided to stand by both points of view and delay the final decision until prevailing conditions changed, since actual reform — any reform — was impossible to implement anyway.[9]

The question of leadership was solved without any prolonged discussion. A. Stulginskis gave way to Father Mykolas Krupavičius who then was elected chairman of the united Central Committee. Among the Committee members were *A. Stulginskis, Father M. Reinys* (later Archbishop of Vilnius), *Dr. P. Karvelis* (later Minister of Finance), *K. Bizauskas* (later Minister of Education, Vice-Premier, Ambassador to the Holy See), and others.

The new governing body began its work under the most trying of circumstances. The provisional government of Lithuania tried desperately to legalize the newly proclaimed independence by securing international recognition. At the same time, the country was waging a valiant war against, not only one, but, three enemies: Soviet Russia, Poland, and a maverick Germanic army. On top of that, the country strove to achieve a measure of normalcy, no mean goal under such circumstances. Trying to address itself to these problems, the new Central Committee was bent on solving the land reform problems. Father Mykolas Krupavičius held lengthy meetings with the then Bishop of Vilnius, Jurgis Matulaitis, a renowned sociologist and theologian. His opinion was cherished not only because of his scholarly authority, but also because of his high office. The Prelate embraced the radical reform plan and added many valuable touches to it. However, the implementation had to wait for several more years, although the refined plan was accepted by all of the Christian Democratic leadership.

74

At the very end of the year (1918), the Red Army managed to approach the outskirts of Vilnius. The Volunteer Lithuanian Army, underfed, underpayed, and underequipped, gave a glorious account of itself and, finally came out victorious, but not before some very close calls. An acute crises developed. The Cabinet presided by the Populist Party statesman, M. Sleževičius, (in which Christian Democrats participated) left the capital city and relocated in Kaunas. On New Year's Eve, the Central Committee also moved to Kaunas and directed all its energies in fighting the enemies.

Since the time was not propitious for any normal internal activity, let alone convening the Constituent Assembly or beginning of an all-encompassing agrarian reform, the government proposed a Conference of State to be held to establish new guidelines for national policies. The Christian Democrats suggested the delegates to be elected by universal, secret, and equal ballot. Other parties however, demurred and prevailed. Membership of the conference was elected by self-governing municipal bodies: 187 delegates in all, 93 of them Christian Democrats.[10] Thus, in fourteen years, (1905-1919), the Christian Democrats evolved into the majority Lithuanian party: in the Grand Congress of Vilnius in 1905, the Christian Democrats were ignored as a political force, whereas, in the State Conference of 1919, they were but a few votes short of an absolute majority. (Forty delegates proclaimed themselves non-partisan, 38 belonged to the Populists and the rest to smaller groups).[11]

The Conference convened on January 16, 1919, and besides the elected delegates, was attended by the State Council and the full Cabinet of the Provisional Government. Although the Christian Democrats had a large representation and could have easily dominated the proceedings, they nevertheless did not choose to dictate terms and resolutions. (This most remarkable and statesmanlike posture was one of the most appealing traits of the party during all the subsequent several years when Christian Democrats had large majorities in the Diet.)

Among the more important decisions were the following: the State Council's and the Cabinet's activities were approved; the Conference reiterated the necessity of convening the Constituent Assembly as well as implementing the land reform; and, the State Council's membership was expanded.[12] (The Chief Executive's functions remained in the Presidium of the Council, however, shortly after the conference, the Council changed this and elected its chairman, A. Smetona, as the first Provisional President of the Republic.)

As a side effect of the Conference, and because of internal disagreement between liberal forces, Prime Minister M. Sleževičius, resigned and a new Cabinet took over presided by the first Christian Democrat as Prime Minister — Pr. Dovydaitis (later most respected scholar and Siberian slave labor camp martyr). His cabinet holds yet another distinction of sorts: that of the shortest tenure of all Lithuanian cabinets — one month.

The ensuing year was marked by the War of Independence and several military victories which assured peaceful progress of a new, reborn nation. The end of hostilities was also crowned with the election and convening of the Constituent Assembly. As far as the Christian Democrats were concerned, this year was also marked by the emergence of two organizations of Christian Democratic persuasion. Both were created as professional, non-political, organizations within the Christian Democratic

76

movement. But both, shortly after inception, entered political life on their own, however, still within the framework of Christian Democracy. This unifying relationship is followed to this day.

The *Labor Federation of Lithuania* was organized in September of 1919 during a meeting of several trade and service organizations representing about 4000 workers. Soon the Federation embraced all Christian labor organizations and Christian trade unionists. Its stated main purpose was to work for social, economic and cultural improvement for the workers. During the democratic period, the Federation grew to around 200,000 members and was well represented in the Lithuanian Diet.[13] (In the 1922 elections, it won 11 seats, in 1923 — 12, and in 1926 — 6 seats.) The main leaders of the Federation were *P. V. Raulinaitis, P. Radzevičius, Dr. K. Ambrozaitis, P. Jočys, Miss M. Avietėnaitė, Prof. Pr. Dovydaitis* (Prime Minister of the third Cabinet), *J. Valaitis, V. Beržinskas* and others. Federation's accomplishments in labor and social legislation were considerable, as was its very successful action against Marxist-Communist infiltration in the Lithuanian labor force.[14]

The *Farmer's Union of Lithuania* was organized during the election to the Constituent Assembly. It evolved from the 18 farmers who were elected on the Christian Democratic slate. Its main purpose was also professional — to represent the interests of Lithuanian agrarian population which, of course, meant the majority of the population. Besides political activity, the Union was also active in agrarian economic field — organizing cooperatives, specialized farm bureaus, import-export offices, credit unions, etc. At its peak, the Union had over 400 chapters. Its renowned leader, as well as first chairman, was *A. Stul-*

ginskis, (himself an agronomist and later President of the Republic). Other notable leaders were *Dr. E. Draugelis, Dr. P. Karvelis, Dr. K. Jokantas, Dr. A. Trimakas, Vyt. Petrulis* and others.

The Lithuanian Diet Palace in Kaunas.

PART IV

CREATION OF A MODERN STATE :
A FULFILLMENT

10

THE CONSTITUENT ASSEMBLY

Among the several questions that the political strata, and indeed the whole population was in general agreement, was the yearning of legalization of the newly won independence. So much so, that the Council of State decided to hold elections to the Constituent Assembly even while the country was fighting on three fronts against determined aggression from without bent on destroying the newly emerging country.

The elections lasted three days — April 14, 15, and 16, 1920. The outcome was not unexpected: out of 112 seats, the Christian Democratic block won 59; the Populist and Social Populist block won 28; and, the Social Democrats won 13. The minority groups (Jews, Poles, and Germans) and non-partisan candidates divided among themselves the few remaining seats.[1] This clear Christian Democratic victory at the polls signified not only the acceptance by the electorate of their progressive and realistic program, but also complimented the party's unrelenting groundwork. Mostly, however, it signified the people's trust in Christian Democracy and its principles.

The first meeting of the newly elected legislative body was held on May 15th under very festive auspices. Not only the brand new legislators, but the whole country was bursting with joy and enthusiasm. (This very enthusiasm together with almost religious fervor for democracy accounted for the fact that the polls attracted slightly more than 90 percent of the eligible voters, a feat seldom achieved even in today's mature democratic societies.) The first to address the august body was the Provisional President, A. Smetona, who after some emotionally charged remarks, rendered not only his resignation but that of the Council of State, the Cabinet, and the Chief of Staff of the Armed Forces. At the very same meeting, A. Stulginskis was elected chairman of the Assembly and immediately rose to read the reaffirmation of the Proclamation of Independence: "The Constituent Assembly of Lithuania, representing the will of the people of Lithuania, proclaims that the Independent State of Lithuania is in existence and, that it is a democratic Republic bound by ethnographic boundaries and free from all political ties which have existed with other nations". The legislators and the gallery which rose along with the Chairman to hear the historic pronouncement, now burst into uncontrolled ovations. Everyone joined in singing the National Anthem.[2] Many a tear of joy was shed, as if to wash away a century of slavery, deprivation, torture and death.

The second meeting elected other officials and the Constitutional Commission, under the chairmanship of

Christian Democrat *A. Tumènas.*[3] On June 20th a temporary Constitution was adopted and Assembly Chairman
A. Stulginskis was elected the new Provisional President.[4]
Thus began six eventful years of Christian Democratic
rule which by any measure was the crowning achievement
of Lithuanian Christian Democracy.

On June 23rd a new Cabinet was approved. It was
headed by one of the Populist leaders, Dr. K. Grinius
(later the third President of the Republic, a respected and
wise statesman). The Cabinet was a coalition group with
only a few Christian Democrats in it.[5]

Thus organized the Assembly plunged into a myriad
of tasks. At the same time, the situation on the battlefields as well as in the interior, started to deteriorate rapidly. The Red Army again occupied the Vilnius region. The
Polish government let it be known that it had no claims
on the ancient Lithuanian capital. The government,
after calling a general mobilization, ordered the army to
recapture Vilnius. However the Suvalkai agreement notwithstanding (in which Poland formally renounced all
claims to Vilnius) the Polish government ordered one of
its generals to march on Vilnius and to seize it. This General Zheligovsky accomplished, while the Polish government steadfastly proclaimed its complete innocence in the
matter. This duplicity was not very convincing to anybody,
especially after the Secret Service uncovered a well organized Polish plan to overthrow the Lithuanian government through a special paramilitary organization acting
within Lithuanian borders. Father M. Krupavičius, the majority leader of the Assembly, proposed to suspend the work
temporarily until the situation improved. Instead of the
full Assembly, the so called Little Assembly, consisting of
only seven members, sat in session from October 22, 1920

Aleksandras Stulginskis
Second President of Lithuania

to January 17, 1921. The Little Assembly worked diligently: it had 43 meetings, reviewed 51 bills, and enacted 25 laws.[6] During this time several members of the Assembly volunteered for military duty in the battlefront and one fell in the battles with Poland.

The Christian Democrat-Populist coalition expired on January 13, 1922 mostly over the educational policies. On February 8th, a new Cabinet was sworn in headed by another non-Christian Democrat, E. Galvanauskas.[7] This Cabinet lasted until the end of the Assembly's tenure. On October 6, 1922 the Constituent Assembly, after 29 months and 257 plenary meetings terminated its work and declared new elections to the first normal Seimas (Diet).[8]

Lithuanian Christian Democratic delegation of the Constituent Assembly.

84

11

THE CONSTITUTION

Among the more than 300 laws passed by the Constituent Assembly, none were more far-reaching and important than the Constitution and the Land Reform Law, both of which were Christian Democratic creations.

Until 1922 Lithuania did not have a Constitution. Since November 2, 1918 the government guided its work by the temporary constitutional by-laws promulgated by the Council of State. On April 4, 1919 these by-laws were expanded to embrace the institution of Presidency. On April 10, 1920 the Constituent Assembly voted into law a temporary Constitution with the main provision of creating a permanent Constitution.[1]

The Constitution of 1922 was adopted by the Assembly on August 6th of that year. It was a modern, progressive, and well conceived document which won praise from constitutional jurists of other nations, as well as from later Lithuanian legal scholars, who had very little use for Christian Democrats. This was significant because the Constitution was basically a Christian Democratic document. It grew out of Christian Democratic precepts and reflected the best of Christian Democracy as well as the best of Lithuanian national spirit and goals.

The work of drafting the document was slow, painful, and at times, stormy. The Commission charged with the job was a coalition group made-up mostly of Christian Democrats and leftists, and chaired by Professor A. Tumėnas, a brilliant jurist. Two other Christian Democrats did an outstanding job. Z. Starkus, although a non-jurist was an extremely capable editorial master (later Minister of Interior). Father K. Šaulys was a professor of Cannon Law and drafted most of the paragraphs having to do with religion and education. The leader of the leftist group was the former Prime Minister, M. Sleževičius.

The final draft was not acceptable either to the Populists or to the Social Democrats. The latter complained bitterly because of clauses having to do with religious matters, religious education in particular, even about God's name in the Preamble. They also demanded the abolition of the death penalty and accused the Christian Democrats of general disregard for the working man. The Populists took exception to religious schools, limited censorship, and, as did the Social Democrats, demanded the abolition of the institution of the Presidency. At the last meeting before the vote, Father Krupavičius addressed himself to those objections and refuted them one by one. He said in part: "This Constitution reflects the will of the people and their most sacred wishes. It safeguards faith of all denominations and guarantees conditions for succeful social and economic development. It safeguards our com-

Msgr. Kazimieras Šaulys, PA

mon people from the leftist yoke of collectivization. The Constitution orients Lithuania towards the West, rejects any class dictatorship and guarantees the widest autonomy for the country's minorities." [2]

When the vote came, 94 Assembly members were present. It was carried by 59 votes. The Populists and the Social Democrats voted present. Only one vote was cast against it.

The Constitution of 1922 has 15 titles and 108 paragraphs covering, as all Constitutions do, the whole spectrum of basic principles. Just as many other revered documents of this type, it begins with "In the name of Almighty God, Lithuanian Nation gratefully acknowledging the sacrifices of her sons..."

Several paragraphs deserve mentioning. Title I stated that the functions of government are divided between the Legislature, the Executive and the Judiciary. (However the power was left mostly in the hands of the legislative branch — typical French-type parliamentarian rule, popular all over Europe at that time). Title II spelled out the rights of the citizens. In 13 clauses the citizens were assured non-discrimination because of race, creed, sex, or national origin. Every citizen was also assured a speedy trial, freedom of religion, press, and organization; the right of petition, to property, etc. Title III specified that the Seimas (Diet) was to be elected every three years by universal, equal, direct and secret ballot. Tile IV was devoted to the Executive. It was to be two-fold: the President and the Cabinet. The President must be not younger than 35 years of age and elected by the Diet by secret ballot. He can be removed from office only by two-thirds vote of all Diet members. The tenure is two three-year periods. If the President becomes incapacitated, his duties are assumed by the Chairman of the Assembly. The Cabinet is organized by the Prime Minister, who in turn is appointed, and gets his mandate from the President. The Cabinet is approved by the President but is responsible to the Diet jointly, and every Minister individually, within the sphere of his responsibilities. Title V spells-out the prerogatives of the independent Judiciary headed by the Supreme Court. Title VI expounds on selfrule of various municipality levels. Title VII in no uncertain language guarantees all the rights and privileges (including educational matters) of the minorities. Title VIII covers national defense, and Title IX educational matters. The two most important and controversial clauses outline the right of private and parochial schools, and the mandatory religion classes in all grade and high schools, with the exception of those private schools which are organized by parents for the express purpose of not including religion (any religion) in the curriculum. Title X covers matters of religious rights and practices. The main point: an absolute freedom of religion. The most important paragraphs in Title XI deal with the inalienable right of private property, the right of business initiative and the State's right to regulate land ownership (to a degree). Title XII establishes the principles of taxes, budgetary laws, and the Office of the State Comptroller. Social security matters are dealt-with in Title XIII. The State is charged with the responsibility of guarding the health and solving other social problems under circumstances beyond individual control: old age, illness, unemployment, injury, etc. (Later specific and very progressive laws covered all Social Security contingencies). Title XIV and Title XV cover procedural matters having to do with ratification, changes and similar objectives.[3]

12

THE LAND REFORM

Another monumental achievement of Lithuanian Christian Democracy was the Land Reform Law and its promulgation. It is indeed a historic accomplishment which not only became a basis for economic development but is internationally recognized as a model law, as well as, a singularly successful agrarian reform. (The late great Christian Democrat, Alcide De Gasperi, on several occasions, publicly praised this land reform as an outstanding achievement, and paid tribute to its principal author and promulgator Father M. Krupavičius).[1]

The matter of land in its problematic totality was always of importance to Christian Democrats. Most of the forerunners of Lithuanian Christian Democracy (the outstanding figures of the Potential Period), never failed to address themselves to this problem. Father Strazdas as well as Bishop Baranauskas, talk about it even in their poems. Their two main contentions were: that the large estates and their hold on serfs was the fount of every misery in Lithuania, and that God never intended this to be so. Thus, it must be changed. The 20th paragraph of the first Christian Democratic program states clearly that: "The estates must return all lands to their rightful peasant owners... The land must be a grant without any renumeration to the unlawful large estate holders".[2] In the Conference of Vilnius (1905) this concern was expressed by a Christian Democrat, Father Aleksandravičius, in his classic statement that "The land belongs to those who till it".[3] Both Christian Democratic conferences of 1917 (in St. Petersburg and Vilnius) deliberated on this matter and evolved the principles and methods to carry it out. These guidelines were approved by the Conference of 1918.[4] On New Year's Eve in 1919, the Central Committee adopted the resolution calling for immediate land reform.[5] This resolution was again reaffirmed by the Central Committee and by the Second State Conference of 1919.[6] Deeds followed words and, the first agrarian law was passed by the Council of State on June 26, 1919.[7] This was only a prelude. It regulated only land grants to the War of Independence volunteers. A number of agrarian laws under Christian Democratic prodding were passed in the first months of the Constituent Asembly: June 28, 1920 a law regulating land sale and grants; July 27, 1920 a law regulating the rents of private farms; August 4, 1920, a new law regulating land grants to the volunteers; August 14, 1920 preliminary Land Reform Act,[8] etc. Other laws followed until on February 15, 1922, The Land Reform Act was passed.

The genesis of land reform had several distinct phases as well as separate spheres of activity. First of interest (and importance) is the way the idea was born and grew in the mind and heart of the author of the reform — Father Mykolas Krupavičius. (This will be dealt with more extensively in a later chapter, outlining Father Krupavičius' life and work.)

Second, as was mentioned before, the land reform thought itself was new neither to the Christian Democrats nor others. (The Populist groups as well as Social Democrats for years also kept thinking about it, although, especially in the case of the Socialists, their ideas were quite different from those of the Christian Democrats.) These divergent opinions soon became the object of heated discussions in the Constituent Assembly. At the very outset, the Social Democrats made it quite clear that they would not support any act which was based on the principle of private property. Nationalization of all land and implements was their goal and they defended it vigorously. (According to one of its representatives: "It is folly to think that we will create a Garden of Eden by tearing the land apart in miniscule plots. No — we will create hell!")[9] The Populist block was somewhat divided on the subject. The majority was leaning towards nationalization although, on more moderate terms and in prolonged phases. The minority was closer to the views of the Christian Democrats. (One of the moderates was A. Rimka, a Populist authority on agrarian problems whose contributions to the reform were considerable.)

The Christian Democratic position was radical, but moderately so. The main principles were: the land must belong to those who till it; the nation will best benefit from successful small landowners whose acreage would be economically feasible; and the distributed land must not only be made available on easy terms to the new owners but, the large estate owners who will lose their

Archbishop Jurgis Matulaitis

lands in the process must be equitably remunerated. In refuting the opposition arguments, the Christian Democratic leadership presented an array of eloquent arguments of their own. *Father J. Staugaitis* (later Bishop), Vice-Chairman of the Assembly, presented the results of a very recent poll according to which 98 percent of all Lithuanian people were in favor of private enterprise and private land ownership.[10] Father Mykolas Krupavičius, in his usually most eloquent discourses, based his argumentation on nothing less than Pope Leo XIII's encyclical, *"Rerum Novarum"*, which states that "It is necessary to refute the Socialist thesis which advocates nationalization by the State of all private property and converting it into public domain".[11] He also very effectively used the doctoral dissertation of the aforementioned Bishop Matulaitis whose subject matter was private ownership and whose conclusions were exactly the same as the previously formulated and now proposed Christian Democratic position.[12]

Opinions were even more widely divergent on the subject of church-owned land. The Social Democrats and the Populist block were unanimous in demanding outright nationalization of all church owned land and appurtenances (buildings, livestock, etc.). The position was clearly discriminatory and the Christian Democrats opposed it vehemently. They reasoned that although the church land should be treated in the same manner as the large estates, it certainly should not be discriminated against. On the other hand, while most of the large estates were owned by foreign absentee landlords, the Lithuanian Church acquired its holdings mostly through grants, which were usually conditioned by various special stipulations of religious nature. Finally, most of the Church holdings, including land, were already nationalized by the Czarist

Msgr. Mykolas Krupavičius in the early twenties

government and now belonged to the State. In that part of Lithuania where such situations existed, the Church should not be further punished but reimbursed for at least the buildings and other property.[13]

All these arguments actually swayed but a few votes. At the final outset, the measure was passed by the votes of Christian Democrats and the lone non-partisan representative. The Social Democrats voted against it and the Populist block, together with the Jewish representatives, abstained.[14]

Third, even the Christian Democratic leadership pushing for the agrarian reform had to be sure it was treading on firm moral grounds. The problem was definitely touchy. On the one hand, the Christian Democrats could not propose and defend such a far-reaching measure if its very propriety could be questioned in terms of the teachings of the Church. On the other hand, Lithuania, a predominantly Catholic nation, would have not accepted anything tainted with insubordination to the Church's teachings. Firm moral and legal understanding was mandatory before attempting a campaign of such importance.

Father Mykolas Krupavičius turned to the very sources of authentic thought. In his book published in 1921 called *"Our Ways"* he dealt extensively with the Church's teachings on the subject, using primarily *"Rerum Novarum"* as a springboard. Trying to justify the Christian Democratic position he reached even further back and quoted extensively from previous Popes and various official documents of the Church. Some of these precepts dated as far back as the XII century, and gathered in Father Krupavičius' treatise, they made a convincing body of thought on the subject. Quoting from Popes Clemens IV, Sixtus

96

IV, Julius II, Pius VI, Pius XI, and others, the author of the Land Reform built an air-tight case for his position. It was an extremely impressive case for land reform and private land ownership. In this, the agrarian architect was also immensely aided by a contemporary authority, the before mentioned Bishop of Vilnius, J. Matulaitis, one of the first sociologists of the time. Father Mykolas Krupavičius quoted the Bishop's writings extensively and they not only made good reading, but also a strong case for an equitable land reform.

Alongside this theological and moral intercourse among the politicians, theologians and laymen in the higher echelons, the very same discussions were waged in lesser circles: Catholic organizations, clergy meetings, and the press. Christian Democrats had to gather around themselves all their wits to convince the influential strata of the population of the rightiousness of their path. Needless to say, the opposition was equally energetic, if less scrupulous. Many of the landowners considered themselves model Catholics and had close friends among influential clergy. On the other hand, the older clergy itself was conservative and not at all geared to accept such a radical departure from the "accepted" social and economic policies. Finally, even some Christian Democratic leaders, as well as other influential Catholic laymen, entertained serious doubts especially about the reimbursement clauses.

The fight was uphill all the way but Christian Democracy scored a victory of immense dimensions. However, the enactment of the measure was only half the battle. The implementation itself was just as prone to obstacles as the enactment of the Act was. Not willing to burden anyone with such a thankless task, Father Krupavičius took the challenge upon himself and assumed the duties of the

Minister of Agriculture. (As the foremost leader of the Party, Father Krupavičius was pressured to accept the Presidency, but never consented to it.) He achieved remarkable results.

The Land Fund consisted of over 724,000 hectares (land belonging to the State, the Czar, banks, private large estates, etc.). (Not counting 600,000 hectares of forests).[15] The law stipulated that all lands above 80 hectares (one Hectare equals 2.48 acres), must be put into the Fund. Some exceptions were made to accommodate model farms, experimental farming stations, etc.). Later the maximum was raised to 150 hectares.[16] Foreign landowners who acquired the acreage in the open market were given three years to sell it in the open market. The former landowners whose lands were to be put into the Fund had the option to choose that part of it, which they wished to keep as their property. Contrary to strong Social Democratic demands not to reimburse the owners for the sequestered land, the government did reimburse for every hectare, paying on the average 27 litai (Lithuanian monetary unit) per hectare. Up until 1935, 343 landowners were thus paid close to 40 million litai.[17]

The bulk of the land distribution was carried out during the tenure of Father Krupavičius. In three years he distributed over 353,000 hectares of land out of total of 554,000 ha distributed in 20 years.[18] Over 39,000 landless tenant farmers and sharecroppers became small landowners. The average land size was just above nine hectares. On top of that, 26,000 very small farmers were given the opportunity to increase their acreage.[19] Thus, the majority of the people who wanted land were accommodated, although the individual acreage was smaller than the reformers anticipated.

The new farmers were not given the land free. However, everything was done to make the repayment as painless as possible. The price per hectare varied considerably, depending on the location and quality of the land (between 18 and 252 litai per hectare). The repayment period was set at the maximum of 36 years. On top of that, many new farmers were extended credit by the Ministry of Agriculture itself or by the Bank of Agriculture. The volunteers of the Wars of Independence were granted land free and were also subsidized by certain quotas of lumber and other building materials.[20]

Along with the land distribution, Father Krupavičius also tackled the other two important aspects of the reform —that of village reorganization and agricultural policy.

Up to that time, a large part of the country was organized on the village-cluster principle which agrarian specialists deemed suited neither for livestock or dairy industry, nor socially desirable. To accommodate the new thrust towards livestock production, the villages were partitioned into separate homesteads. This phase was also carried out expeditiously and although never completely finished, it had a tremendous impact on agricultural economy.

Change to a different product policy proved to be equally beneficial. For several centuries, Lithuanian farming was based on the so-called three-field system: one-third was fallow land, one-third sown with winter grain, and the last third was spring grain and plantings. The Russian agriculture was in an even worse situation and naturally during the occupation years, Lithuanian farming did not progress. Only enough was produced to satisfy the internal demand. All this changed after World War I. Since the grain market was already saturated with the

Danube countries' products, the reform architects wisely decided to concentrate on live-stock production. Partition of villages to a great degree aided in this policy change. The predominant three-field system gave way to the 6-10 system or the Norfolk four-field plan. At the same time, mineral fertilization was introduced, agriculture machinery acquired, and farming education initiated. Soon, Lithuanian dairy and livestock products were internationally known. (As a matter of fact, just before World War II, Lithuania produced 110 per cent of the food products necessary for internal consumption.)[21]

These few remarks cannot even begin to describe either the philosophy of land reform or the monumental undertaking which was necessary to carry it out. Sufficient to say that the Act itself, as well as its promulgation, was done in a most exemplary manner. True, some countries at that time carried out even more radical agrarian reforms, but Lithuanian enterprise won international acclaim for its fairness, good planning, and exemplary execution. During the process, many farming specialists from as far away as the United States and India visited Lithuania to observe the procedures and processes involved. As a matter of fact, there are more books written in foreign languages about the Lithuanian Land Reform than there are in Lithuanian. Christian Democrats are justifiably proud of this achievment. In the words of the late *Archbishop P. Karevičius,* "Christian Democrats built themselves a monument that will stand for ages, and earned the gratitude of the entire nation".[22] But the final judgment was rendered by the people themselves. As the Lithuanian farm economy prospered and grew from year to year by leaps and bounds, Christian Democrats knew that their toil was worth all the sacrifices. This, of course, was the ultimate justification of it all.[23]

100

13

THE FIRST AND SECOND DIETS

The elections to the first regular Seimas (Diet) were quite different from previous elections. The split between the Christian Democrat and the Populist blocks could not be healed; it actually was deepening and widening. The divergent opinions concerning the Constitution, the land reform, and the educational system, etc. were driving the partners apart. This was unfortunate because the coalition was beneficial to the country's political life. The Populist block (soon both Populist parties — the Populists and the Social Populists — merged into one Party) [1] more and more sided with the Social Democrats. In that sense, the camps were more clearly defined than before.

The leftist groups did everything possible to unseat the Christian Democrats whom they by now wholeheartedly disliked. The Christian Democrats, however, were not ready to give up the power needed to implement their ideas, which they cherished for so long. The campaign was fierce and at times undignified. Both sides sometimes overstepped the limits of gentlemanly politiking. After the balloting was over, the Christian Democrats registered another victory. Out of 78 representatives, they won 38.[2] Even the leftist block and the minority candidates together could not muster a majority. The opposition was even weaker because some minority seats were held by people whom even the Populist-Socialist coalition did not trust.

The Christian Democrats tried to woo back the Populists into yet another coalition government, but to no avail. The tension would not let up and the whole work of the Diet suffered as a consequence. The magic of the Consituent Assembly was losing much of its luster.

The first major order of business was carried out only in the 14th meeting when the Diet re-elected A. Stulginskis as President of the Republic.[3] In the meantime, the Prime Minister complained bitterly about a "do nothing" Diet which in his opinion, hindered the progress of reconstruction.[4] Indeed, arguments abounded about everything, even the leadership of the Diet itself, but very little was actually accomplished. However, even this short-lived (only four months) Diet had its moment of glory. It came on January 23, 1923, in the 20th meeting, when Prime Minister E. Galvanauskas informed the Diet of a communication the government had received from the Supreme Council of Lithuania Minor, requesting it to be annexed to the Lithuanian Republic.[5] (The question at hand was actually only the Klaipėda-Memel region which was first occupied by Germany, than provisionally governed by the Entante. Germany and Poland did everything possible to grab this ancient Lithuanian port city and ter-

102

The leadership of the CD Parliamentary Delegation in the early twenties. Second from left - one time Chairman of the LCDP and later President of the Republic Aleksandras Stulginskis, third - longtime Party Chairman Mykolas Krupavičius.

ritory for themselves. However, the Lithuanians of the region in popular insurrection, aided by volunteer forces from Lithuania, managed to oust all invaders.). The whole Lithuania Minor, a much larger territory, for centuries a part of ethnographic Lithuania, stayed in the hands of the Germans until after World War II and since, is annexed to the Russian Federated Socialist Republic — the largest of the so-called republics of USSR).

During the ensuing speeches, leaders of every party endorsed the request, and the Diet itself, in a special resolution, ordered the government to explore all avenues of action to incorporate the region into the Republic. A month later, the Prime Minister informed the Diet that the Lithuanian Army was deployed in the region and Lithuanian tri-color was flying all over this ancient Lithuanian countryside.[6]

On March 13, 1923, the Diet was dissolved by the President and new elections were announced to take place on May 12th and 13th next.[7]

The campaign was no less heated this time. The Christian Democrats again came out victors. Out of 78 seats, they managed to win 40. The now united Populists lost heavily and elected only 16 representatives. Social Democrats also lost and had to be content with only eight. Communist-leaning Labor group which in the second Diet managed to grab five seats, now lost all five. The biggest gains were registered by the minorities — Jewish increased their seats from four to seven. Other groups also gained.[8] This Diet was the most productive and lived out its tenure.

The newly victorious Christian Democrats this time took a firm hand in organizing the Diet. On June 19th, A. Stulginskis was again re-elected President. On June 30th Prime Minister E. Galvanauskas and his Cabinet were approved. After strong bidding from the Christian Democrats, the Populists again entered into a coalition with the ruling party. However, the previous spirit was not resurrected. The Populists proved to be less than enthusiastic supporters of government policies. On the other hand, the Christian Democrats were not willing to give in to minority whims as much as before. A year later (on June 18, 1924) a new Cabinet was formed with A. *Tumėnas* (a Christian Democrat) as Prime Minister.[9] While the Christian Democrats stubbornly pushed their extensive program forward, the leftist mounted an increasingly stronger opposition. Every accomplishment was preceded by heated debates, charges and countercharges. To realign their forces, the Christian Democrats, on February 3, 1925, reorganized the Cabinet. The post of Prime Minister was given to *V. Petrulis*.[10] Only seven months later, he gave way to *Dr. L. Bistras*.[11] On February 26, 1926, the Diet pulled a switch on the Christian Democrats and elected as its new chairman a Populist, Dr. J. Staugaitis.[12] However, the relations between the two largest parties did not improve. On March 26, 1926, the Diet held its last meeting, the 246th. New elections were announced for May 8th and 9th.[13] The Christian Democrats did not realize that a surprise was in the political wind.

14

OTHER ACHIEVEMENTS

Six years in the life of a nation is really a very brief time. However, during those six years Christian Democrats not only built up a country, but created a basis upon which the resurrected nation erected a monume'al national structure.

The Constitution and the Land Reform, deeds of historic dimensions, were but two of many achievements. The newly independent country was bursting with energy and the Christian Democrats channeled it in the most beneficial way.

Of primary importance was the restructuring of the educational system. The Czarist legacy in this field was extremely impoverished — the oppressors were not at all interested in the education of a nation which was to be dissolved into the all-embracing Russian melting pot anyway. Every facet of education was in want: teachers were scarce, money even more so; the educational plant non-existent;

and, textbooks were outmoded, few in number and variety, etc. On top of all that, the Constituent Assembly could not agree on educational philosophy to be incorporated into the Constitution.

The Christian Democrats had a firm and well thought out program. The primary and secondary education must be under the State's control; various municipalities, organizations and groups of citizens must have a right to organize private schools; religion must be a part of the curriculum; and, the State University must have state-supported colleges for Catholic and Protestant theology.[1]

The Social Democrats and to a lesser degree the Populists, were in strong opposition on all four points. To the Marxist-oriented Socialists, religious instruction was out of the question altogether. The Populist position was not much different. Both parties were against private schools, as well as the theological colleges. Thus, only State supervision was a point on which all agreed, but even there, unanimity was on principle only.[2] In the end, the Christian Democratic viewpoint prevailed, and although it was politically damaging to the Christian Democratic-Populist Coalition, the system itself paved the way for an outstanding network of high caliber schools. The Grade School Act was passed on October 6, 1922.[3] Just six months earlier with the President of the Republic in attendance, the University of Kaunas was established, later to be known as Vytautas the Great University. Thus, after 90 years, Lithuania again had a university which soon developed into a respected center of higher education, comparable to many Western schools. To aid agriculture, a whole array of specialized schools were organized. Among them: The Agriculture Academy, three Higher Agricultural Education schools, six Lower Agricultural Education schools and 58 Agricultural Clinics. To aid farmers, 29 special technical books were published and a newspaper established which reached a circulation of 80,000 and was mailed free of charge.[4] Its main purpose — to help the farming population with technical and general education.

On July 21, 1922, the State School of Art was established. A year later, a Conservatory of Music followed. In the same period, an Officer Candidate School was organized, as well as a General Staff School. Soon after the convening of the Constituent Assembly, a later renowned M. K. Čiurlionis Art Gallery was established. At the same time, State Archives Office was organized and Government Printing Office established.

Noteworthy gains were also made in the field of economy in general. Of primary importance was the complete re-organization of the monetary system, with Litas as a monetary unit, which for the remainder of the independence years, was a highly regarded currency internationally for its stability. Along with the Bank of Lithuania (the central bank), several other banks were established (among them — Credit Bank of Lithuania, National Bank, Cooperative Bank, and Bank of Agriculute, etc.).

In the field of agriculture (Lithuania was predominantly agricultural), the following samples illustrate the economic thrust forward. In six years the Christian Democratic Government established: 278 animal husbandry centers, 280 grain processing centers, 23 fruit and vegetable centers, 266 milk processing firms, 194 dairy firms, 46 flak processing centers, 2 grain elevators, etc.[5] The first co-operative laws were also passed during this period.

108

Basic social security legislation was also of Christian Democratic authorship. Although several important laws regulating working hours and other labor matters were enacted by the State Council, most of the important legislation was passed by the Constituent Assembly and succeeding Diets. In 1921 — Farm Laborers Hiring Law and Industrial Workers Compensation Law; in 1922 — Civil Service Salary Act; in 1924 — Estate Labor Hiring Act; in 1925 — Labor Inspection Law, Soldier's Pension Law, and Paid Holiday Act; and, in 1926 — Government Workers' Pension Law, Social Security Law (establishing also the Central Social Security Office), Sick Benefits Funds Law, etc. These are but a few of an array of laws in this field.

This parliamentary period dominated by the Christian Democrats saw also the relations between Lithuania and the Holy See take a new direction. Paradoxically, it was an achievement of a rather mixed quality. On the one hand, by the decree of Pope Pius XI (Lituanorum Gente) Lithuanian Province of the Church was established on April 4, 1926. (Up to that time, the several Lithuanian dioceses belonged to various other provinces.) On the other hand, Lithuanians were incensed about the Vatican's refusal to include in the Province's jurisdiction the See of Vilnius, after the city and the region was forcibly occupied and held by Poland. This action brought strong diplomatic exchanges between the Vatican and Lithuania, and consequent relations between the two warmed only slowly.

During the Christian Democratic period, the foundations for Lithuania's foreign policy were laid. It had to be a basically new creation, since Lithuania, the empire of the Middle Ages, was no more. Only geopolitical situation remained the same after the end of World War I. Everything else had changed drastically. Lithuanians early realized that their main foreign policy objective must be normalization of the relationship with three of her neighbors: Soviet Union, Germany, and Poland. Small, civilized, and democratic Latvia to the north had close historic and blood ties with Lithuania, and at no time presented a problem. After the signing of a treaty with Latvia on October 8, 1920, concerning boundaries, etc. both countries maintained warm and friendly relations.

Quite a different relationship existed with the other neighbors. Germany, at least at that time, presented the least problem. Internal situations after the war debacle removed her from the world scene. "Drang nach Osten" was by necessity forgotten. However, Germany still held a considerable part of ethnographic Lithuania (Lithuania Minor) in her clutches and did not intend to give it up. Lithuania, of course, was in no position to enforce her demands. On the other hand, Germany was the first country to recognize Lithuania de jure. Thus, during the ensuing years the relations with Germany were normal, although Lithuania never gave up on its demands to re-unite all Lithuanian lands in one entity.

Russian problem was threefold. On the one hand, she was an age-old Lithuanian oppressor and exploiter. On the other — the revolution changed the Russian collosus immensely. Finally, the Bolshevik Red Army was waging war against Lithuania, even as the Constituent Assembly met to lay the cornerstone of the new Republic. Under such circumstances the normalization of relations was of primary importance. However, Lithuanian military victories on the battlefield and Soviet Union's internal situation facilitated Lithuanian efforts. On July 12, 1920, the two countries signed a Peace Treaty in which the Soviet government relinquished all territorial claims on Lithuania for all times. Article I of the Treaty reads as follows: "Proceeding from the right, proclaimed by the Russian Socialist Federated Soviet Republics, of all nations to free self-determination up to their complete separation from the State into the composition of which they enter, Russia recognized without reservation the sovereign rights and independence of the Lithuanian state, with all the juridical consequences arising from such recognition and voluntarily and for all time abandon all sovereign rights of Russia over Lithuanian people and their territory."

"The fact of the past subjugation of Lithuania to Russia does not impose on the Lithuanian nation and its territory any liabilities whatsoever towards Russia."[6]

The relations were further cemented by the Treaty of Non-Aggression of September 28, 1926, which reads in part: "The relations between the Union of Soviet Socialist Republic and the Lithuanian Republic shall continue to be based on the Treaty of Peace between Lithuania and Russia, concluded at Moscow on July 12, 1920, and all provisions of which shall retain their force and inviolability."[7] And further on — "The Lithuanian Republic and the Union of Soviet Socialist Republic undertake to respect in all circumstances each others sovereignty and territorial integrity and inviolability." [8] (It is characteristic of the Kremlin that only three days after the Peace Treaty was signed, the Red Army entered Vilnius. However, it shortly withdrew to the borders stipulated in the Treaty.) The ensuing relations with USSR were relatively friendly until World War II.

The worst foreign policy problem was presented by Poland, the former partner of Lithuanian-Polish Com-

111

monwealth. The Poles never relinquished their self-pro-
mulgated rights to Lithuania and did everything possible,
including subversion and war, to achieve their goal. The
hostilities were terminated only by the Treaty of Suvalkai
which was primarily an armistice agreement. It was signed
on October 7, 1920, by both countries with English, Italian, and American observers in attendance. By it, a temporary Demarcation Line was established, pending final
treaty which was to follow. However, the very same day,
by order of Poland's Chief of State, Marshall Pilsudsky, the
Polish Army led by General Zheligovsky, overran the
agreed line, and the next day, overpowered the Lithuanians in Vilnius. This seizure was not only a treacherous
act in itself, but it was also in violation of the Allied policy
laid down on July 10, 1920, at the Spaa Conference. At the
same time, it also disregarded the provisions of the Curzon
line which stipulated that Vilnius and Gardinas are to
stay in Lithuanian territory. It was also against the better
judgment of Great Britain and The League of Nations,
both of which, together with the majority of the European
Press, condemned this Polish coup de force.

In the renewed hostilities, Lithuania in several key
battles, roundly defeated the Polish Army. Only the Allied intervention prevented Lithuanians from recapturing
the capital city. On November 29, 1920, pressured by the
Allies, Lithuania signed yet another armistice agreement.
Three years later, on March 15, 1923, Polish diplomats
managed to convince the Conference of Ambassadors and
secured recognition of the fait accompli. Thus, Vilnius,
and about a third of Lithuanian territory, stayed occupied
by Poland, although the city for more than 600 years
was the capital of Lithuania.[9]

Under such circumstances, Lithuania hermetically
sealed its borders with Poland and until the eve of World

War II, no diplomatic or other relations existed between the two countries.[10]

The fourth problem — that of gaining recognition by the International Community was overcome by unending and deft diplomatic activity. On September 22, 1921, Lithuania became a member of The League of Nations. By November of 1924, the Christian Democratic government secured de facto and de jure recognition from all the Big Powers and over forty other countries.[11]

It is only fair to state that all these accomplishments were by no means the sole work of the Lithuanian Christian Democratic Party. Uncounted thousands of martyrs lost their lives during the century of oppression. Thousands more vanguished in Siberian prisons. Many sacrificed their lifetimes in pursuit of freedom. Many volunteers died on the battlefronts at the very same time that Lithuania was taking her first independent steps. Even in political terms all political parties, especially the Populists, did their best in aiding to build the new country. Indeed, every Lithuanian citizen throughout the land sacrificed a great deal for the betterment of all. The national accomplishment was only the sum of every citizen's contribution to his country. However, as the guides of Lithuania's destiny in the years of resurrection, the Christian Democrats were in the forefront of the march. Many a legislative act or administrative decision of importance was theirs and theirs alone. They accepted the challenge and the mandate, they took the risks of unpopular decisions and, many times they staked their reputations in the parliamentary debates and ballots. Theirs to a great degree is also the credit. They proved the viability of Christian Democracy and the creativity and industriousness of the common man. By doing that, they built on the ruins of a great empire of the Middle Ages, a modern, prosperous, and viable nation.

PART V

PROFILES IN ACTION:
THE LEADERS OF AN ERA

15

MYKOLAS KRUPAVIČIUS— A BUILDER OF A NATION

Christian Democracy found many fertile minds among the Lithuanians. Many a Christian Democratic idea was born in magnanimous hearts even before Christian Democracy appeared on the social and political horizon. Some of the names were mentioned in previous chapters. None of them were statesmen or politicians, although given a different set of circumstances, some of them would have become great political innovators. Most of them were priests, men of letters, and deeply Christian social reformers.

The later generation of Christian Democrats were not only steeped in Christian Democratic ideals and ideas, but also were given a chance to flourish in political life and in the affairs of state. Many of these became highly sophisticated politicians, creative statesmen, and first class diplomats.

Msgr. Mykolas Krupavičius

None of them, however, can match the dedication, the vigor, the political ecumen or the statesman's qualities of Mykolas Krupavičius. (1885-1970) His labors in Christian Democracy have earned him the patriarchal title of "The Father of Lithuanian Christian Democracy". To his last days, Father Krupavičius, was active in Lithuanian Christian Democratic circles. His counsel was eagerly sought by the younger leaders of the exile movement, and he was universally revered as one of the greatest living Lithuanians.

Mykolas Krupavičius was an immensely talented person and an extraordinary personality. At the same time, he possessed the uncanny simplicity so characteristic of great men. And again, there was a touch of contradiction about him which does not lend itself to an easy explanation.

First and foremost, Mykolas Krupavičius was a Catholic priest.[1] (Some years ago he was elevated to the rank of Prelatus Domesticus of the Papal Court, but characteristically prefered to be addressed simply as Priest.) Therein lies one of the seeming contradictions. Although most of his life was spent in politics, administration, diplomacy, conspiracy and similar rather unpriestly occupations, he always remained a most devoted, very religious and consciencious servant of God. Even the greatest affairs of state or the most pressing political crises did not sway him from his daily priestly duties which he performed diligently to his last days. The Holy Sacrament of Priesthood and his person were actually fused into one most human, and at the same time, most spiritual entity.

On the other hand, this finely tuned personality was wrapped within the purest Lithuanian shroud. Lithuanianism to him was much more than formal citizenship

118

or sentimental attachment. It was a religiously inspired calling, willed by God and freely embraced by a man. In matters Lithuanian, Father Krupavičius was indeed of granite strength. If anything brought poetry to his rather reserved personality, it was Lithuanian affairs: the country's sufferings, her misfortunes, her glorious past, and hopeful future.

So did Christian Democracy. He was the one who raised Lithuanian Christian Democracy from a rather loose confederation of ideas and people to an instrument of social justice and political power. In Christian Democracy he saw the one social and political system which can truly change not only a man's fate, but the very face of a nation. He used it with a master's touch and with a wise man's sophistication. In his actions, Christian Democracy was a live instrument of infinite variability and effectiveness. His great intellect opened new avenues in the precepts which are as old as Christianity itself. In this sense, Father Krupavičius stands among the greatest prophets of Christian Democracy since it unfolded itself out of the depths of the Gospel and the heights of the Sermon on the Mount.

His biographical sketch unfolds a portrait of a man of mosaic beauty and brilliance.

Mykolas Krupavičius was born on October 1, 1885, of an impoverished peasant family. His father, striving for a better life tried various trades (even learned beer brewing in Belgium) and finally decided to try his luck in the United States where, after an automobile accident, he died. Raised by a hard-working mother, young Krupavičius early tasted the life of a common laborer. Fascinated by the blacksmith's trade, the youngster was seriously considering taking it up, and only his mother's prodding and advice from an acquaintance, turned him towards a teaching profession. After graduation from the Teachers College at Veiveriai in 1905, young Krupavičius, for several years, taught school at various Polish and Lithuanian towns. However, the young teacher more and more turned his heart towards the religious life for which he felt a calling since early youth. After graduation from the Priest Seminary in Seinai in 1913, the next year he entered the Priesthood, and as a promising student, was sent to the Theological Academy in St. Petersburg from which he graduated in 1917. After a year as a chaplain of the Lithuanian high school in Russian Voronezh, he was informed that, because of his Lithuanian activities, the Bolsheviks had sentenced him to death in absentia. Secretly, by circuitous routes, dressed as a Russian soldier and aided by young Christian Democratic followers, Mykolas Krupavičius reached Lithuanian soil, only to be arrested by the then ruling Germans. After several months of house arrest, helped by Father Staugaitis, (later signer of the Declaration of Independence and a Bishop), he was assigned special duties on the staff of the State Council. A year later, he became special officer of the social program in the Ministry of Interior from which he transferred to the Ministry of Agriculture as a secretary of the Land Reform planning Commission. From 1920 to 1926 he was elected to all the Diets and in 1923-1926 was Minister of Agriculture.

After the Nationalist coup d'etat he was elected first Vice-Chairman of the last democratic Diet which was soon dissolved. In 1927-1929 he studied sociology, economics, journalism, and law at several French universities. Later Father Krupavičius returned to pastoral duties and until 1942, was pastor of several parishes in his home region. Escaping Communist persecution after the Russian invasion in 1940, he was arrested by the subsequent German occupation forces, deported to Germany and held in house arrest until the end of the War. In 1945 , he was elected Chairman of the Supreme Committee for the Liberation of Lithuania (VLIK) and for ten years, crisscrossed the world gathering Lithuanian forces and seeking aid for the liberation cause.

Father Krupavičius' interest in civic and political action demonstrated itself early in his youth. While still in grade school, he distributed forbidden Lithuanian newspapers and books among his neighbors. While teaching, he joined a revolutionary movement and was twice arrested by the Czarist gendarmes. While teaching at another school, he joined the peasants in demanding better living conditions. For this he lost his job and was dragged to the Russian court. During his studies at the Priest Seminary he actively propagated Lithuanianism, was constantly reprimanded by Polish professors and barely escaped dismissal. With every new persecution, Father Krupavičius became more stubborn and more active. In St. Petersburg, he not only belonged to a secret Lithuanian group in the Theological Academy, but was a staff member of a youth magazine, leading member of a workers' society and for a while, president of an organization to aid war refugees.

Father Krupavičius was also one of the organizers of a Lithuanian youth organization "Ateitis" (The Future) which later played an immense role in the life of Lithuanian youth.

In his politics, Father Krupavičius, from the very beginning, embraced Christian Democracy. To him it was the best tool available to change the grinding plight of common men: workers and peasants. During World War

Msgr. Mykolas Krupavičius. Portrait by A. Varnas

I, while in Russia, he became the leader of numerous Christian Democrats and to his last days was the guiding light of Lithuanian Christian Democracy. During the two years prior to the Constituent Assembly, he crisscrossed the Lithuanian countryside visiting every city, town and village organizing public opinion in favor of independence wars, and collecting money needed to support the volunteers in the battlefields. During the campaign to the Constituent Assembly, he again traveled the width and breadth of the country, this time organizing Christian Democrats and putting his party's program forth to anyone who would listen. If Christian Democrats during the three elections won absolute majorities, it was no one else's but Father Krupavičius' doing.

His statesmanship and political genius really shone during those six democratic years at the beginning of Lithuania's independent years. As an orator, he had few peers. His speeches were classic in their simplicity and unassailable logic, sometimes with a touch of irony and sarcasm but, always fair and charitable to his opponents.[2]

As party chairman and majority leader in the Diet, his was the responsibility for ultimate decisions which so vitally affected the politics, policies, and programs of the government, indeed the very lives of every citizen. He carried out these responsibilities with magnificent devotion to the interests of all, with unfailing faith and, with a great deal of greatness.

It was at this time that the government circles, his political friends, and the country at large began to notice his personal traits and his many talents. We already mentioned his oratorical capability. Soon everyone learned of his complete devotion to the country and its people. His love for Lithuania was overpowering. Outwardly, a somewhat distant and reserved person, he nevertheless was charitable to a fault in the best sense of the word. Money played no role in his life — he was a perpetual donor to any and every cause. In private life, he was modest, frugal, and unassuming. He could be a fierce political foe, but never failed to seek compromise, and indeed found it time and time again, where most others never looked. And again, in matters of principle, he was as unbending as a centuries-old Lithuanian Oak. His fidelity to principles was legendary and he never sacrificed anything to compromise it.

Father Krupavičius never changed. Deeply hurt and disappointed by democracy's demise in his beloved country, he left the highest government positions and for years lived among his parishioners as one of them, preaching, teaching, admonishing, and always fighting for Christianity, Democracy, and Christian Democracy.

The same outstanding personal qualities guided his work when he again was called to assume the highest political office as Chairman of the Supreme Committee for Liberation of Lithuania. For ten years, sometimes single-handedly, he kept the institution on course. The going was not easy — it never is in exile.

All along, Father Krupavičius was also a prolific writer. (To the very end he contributed articles to several journals and newspapers.) Among literally uncounted articles, he has close to twenty books to his credit, mostly dealing with Christian Democracy and Sociology. His versatility was demonstrated by the fact that his last book was a monumental work on pastoral theology *"A Priest in the Service of God and People."* [3]

If any one achievement is connected with Father Krupavičius' name and work, it is that of the land reform,

Msgr. M. Krupavičius among young Christian Democrats in Michagan in the early sixties.

and truly so. We already dwelt on several aspects of this historic undertaking. Father Krupavičius was its author, promulgator, and guiding hand. To him, land reform was an intensely personal commitment. This to a great degree explains his all-consuming dedication to the task. Two basic beliefs motivated him.

First, he was himself of common stock, intimately familiar with grinding poverty. This personal experience, even in childhood, was strengthened by his grandfather, whose tales of by-gone days the young child loved and cherished. In most of those stories, the villain was always the large estate holder, the lord of the mansion, the cruel overseer of the poor serfs. It was not unusal for a child to be fascinated by such rather sad tales. What was unusual, was that the child never forgot the subtle lessons and the sociological implications.

Secondly, Father Krupavičius already was at that time, a sociologist of great depth and deep sense of justice. He related personally to poverty and deprivation. It was much more than a political program or intellectual realization. Poverty to him was not a natural state of affairs, but a consequence of injustice. As a totally committed Christian, he could neither justify it nor excuse it. To him, individual poverty superceded national priorities, just as man supercedes the state.

These two forces gave impetus to his actions. This inner strength was also aided by his thorough study of "Rerum Novarum" and related authoritative books on the subject.

This explains his land reform activities. He never once doubted the necessity or legality of it. His knowledge of the nuances of the subject matter was extensive, and he knew he was on sure ground. At the same time, when obstacles were seemingly unsurmountable, his fidelity to principle sustained him. The result, of course, was far more reaching than the architect himself allowed to hope. Serving justice and alleviating individual poverty, Father Krupavičius also built up the national economy. Many factors aided in this process, but his dedication was the catalyst which opened the gates to prosperity.

This was Mykolas Krupavičius, a man among men, and yet a giant. A master of many destinies, and yet a servant of God and man.[4]

16

A GALLERY OF STATESMEN

The challenge of the times created many more men of dedication, wisdom, and action. Only a few can be mentioned although many deserve to be.

Aleksandras Stulginskis (1885-1969) signer of the Declaration of Independence. Of peasant stock, he graduated from the priest seminary but changed his mind about the priesthood, and, after extensive schooling, became an agronomist. He was one of the handful of creators of the Christian Democratic Party and later the leader of the Farmers' Union. From his youth a dedicated patriot, he soon gained prominence as an astute politician and national leader. After hard work in the State Council, A. Stulginskis was elected the first Constitutional President of the Republic and twice was re-elected to his country's highest office. Only 35 years old when first elected Chief of State, A. Stulginskis carried out his duties with dignity

Dr. Leonas Bistras

and wisdom rarely displayed in so young a man. His love for democracy and justice is legendary. During the restrited democracy period (1927-1939), he lived on a farm and worked at it many a day himself. During the first Soviet occupation, he and his wife were deported to Siberia where he was held at several slave labor camps for 13 years. In 1952, he was sentenced by the Soviets to 25 years in prison, but the sentence was commuted after Stalin's death. From 1956 until his death, A. Stulginskis lived in occupied Lithuania and was held in great esteem by all. To Lithuanians on both sides of the Iron Curtain, A. Stulginskis was a symbol of unselfish patriotism, Christian humanism, and unconquerable Lithuanian spirit.

Jurgis Matulaitis-Matulevičius (1871-1927), Archbishop of Vilnius, Apostolic Delegate to Lithuania, and Superior General of The Marian Congregation. Although he formally neither belonged to the party nor was he active in politics, Archbishop Matulaitis was a committed Christian Democrat in the original and larger sense. Because of his great intellect and sociological scholarship, he was often consulted by the leadership of the Party and always gave wise and balanced counsel. An authority on property and its various aspects, the Archbishop gave invaluable assistance to Father Krupavičius on the subject. A holy man, Archbishop Matulaitis is now a candidate for Sainthood.[2]

Leonas Bistras (1890-1971) a laborer's son, philosopher, statesman, politician, journalist, and teacher. A talented and versatile man, Dr. Bistras joined the Christian Democrats in 1910. Later, he was one of the key men in the Party and government. Several times chairman of the Central Committee, he was almost continuously a member from the very beginning. During the Christian Demo-

Kazys Bizauskas

cratic regime, he occupied the highest governmental positions: Chairman of the Diet, Prime Minister, Minister of Foreign Affairs, Minister of Interior, and the Minister of Education. After the coup d'etat, he again briefly served as Minister of Education. Again briefly and in the same post, Dr. Bistras served in the 1939 Coalition Cabinet. Arrested by the Soviets in 1941, Dr. Bistras was deported to the Siberian slave labor camps, tortured, and twelve years later released. He was one of the ablest Christian Democratic leaders and statesmen.[3]

Justinas Staugaitis (1866-1943), Bishop of Telšiai, statesman, writer, and a signer of the Declaration of Independence. A great patriot and civic-minded organizer, the than Father Staugaitis joined the Christian Democratic movement early in life and was a member of the Central Committee. As a member of the State Council, Father Staugaitis undertook several successful diplomatic missions. He was Christian Democratic representative in all but the last democratic Diet; its vice-chairman and chairman. In this capacity, several times he was acting Chief of State. After consecration, Bishop Staugaitis devoted his considerable talents to his diocese and to writing. In both fields he achieved lasting results. His contributions to Lithuanian life are extensive. He loved his country dearly and his last words were: "God do not forsake Lithuania".[4]

Juozas Vailokaitis (1880-1953) priest, civic leader, and economist. Father Vailokaitis was the first chairman of the Lithuanian Christian Democratic Party Central Committee in St. Petersburg. Since early youth, he was active in Lithuanian freedom activities. For that, numerous times punished by the Czarist government and dismissed from the priest seminary. An outstanding economist and businessman, Father Vailokaitis in later years, concentrated in the economic field, especially banking. His was an

Bishop Justinas Staugaitis

outstanding contribution to the budding Lithuanian industry. A generous man, Father Vailokaitis donated considerable sums of money to various causes, especially scholarships to hundreds of university students. After a dozen years in Soviet slave labor camps in Siberia, Father Vailokaitis returned to his beloved country an ill man where he soon died.[5]

Kazimieras Šaulys (1872-1964) a signer of the Declaration of Independence, statesman, canon lawyer, administrator, and Protonotary Apostolic. Monsignor Šaulys was one of the first writers on Lithuanian Christian Democracy and an early member of the movement. An urbane intellectual, Monsignor Šaulys since early youth was active in Lithuanian affairs. As a member of the Constituent Assembly, he was the main author of parts of the Constitution. During the same period, he was also a member of the Central Committee. In later life, Monsignor Šaulys did an outstanding job as the key aid to the Archbishop of Kaunas, and as a long term member of the Executive Council of the Lithuanian Red Cross.[6]

Jonas Vailokaitis (1886-1944) a signer of the Declaration of Independence, financier, and industrialist. Together with his brother, the Reverend Juozas Vailokaitis, he has had lasting influence on Lithuanian banking and industry.[7]

Kazys Bizauskas (born in 1893) a signer of the Declaration of Independence and a diplomat. Member of the State Council and representative in the Diet, Kazys Bizauskas won lasting recognition as the reformer of the educational system during his tenure as Minister of Education. Later, Minister to the Holy See, the Haag, Riga, and Vice-Premier in the Coalition Cabinet of 1939. Deported by the Soviets to the Siberian slave labor camps in 1941, he was never heard from again.[8]

Vytautas Endziulaitis (1893-1918). Although he died in his youth, Vytautas Endziulaitis was already a man of accomplishment. He was one of the authors of the Christian Democratic program of 1917, a leading labor leader of his time, and an organizer of the Labor Federation of Lithuania and the Center of Catholic Action. His untimely death cut short a very promising career.[9]

Antanas Tumėnas (1880-1946) lawyer, statesman, university professor, and civic leader. His most lasting contribution was the first Constitution which was mostly his work. He was the "legal soul" of the democratic period. Minister of Justice and Prime Minister. An erudite jurist, he was also a respected legal and constitutional arbiter. Later, Antanas Tumėnas lectured on Constitutional Law at the University of Kaunas until he was dismissed for his unbending democratic views. After that, he joined private practice and was one of the most respected attorneys of his time. At the same time, he was for many years the head of the Catholic Action organization. During the German occupation, Antanas Tumėnas was one of the original members of the Supreme Committee for Liberation of Lithuania for which he was incarcerated by the Nazi occupation forces. Accused of high treason, he faced a death sentence but his ill health and the oncoming battlefront saved him. He later died in political exile in Austria.[10]

Pranas Dovydaitis (1886-1942) intellectual, youth leader, editor, journalist, and academician. A rough-edged but saintly man, Professor Dovydaitis was active in politics only a short time. A member of the State Council, he was also a signer of the Declaration of Independence and was later Prime Minister. He is credited with the creation of the Lithuanian youth organization "Ateitis" (The Fu-

Bishop Kazimieras Paltarokas

ture). After his short sojourn with politics, he taught at the University of Kaunas and was one of the most active and productive Catholic leaders of the encyclopedist type. Deported to a Siberian slave labor camp, he died there as a martyr never failing to bear witness to his faith and principles.[11]

Mečislovas Reinys (1884-1953) Archbishop of Vilnius, academician and psychologist. A fighter of justice, he saw persecution and prison even in his youth. An active Christian Democrat, he was Minister of Foreign Affairs. After becoming Bishop, he concentrated on pastoral duties and scholarly affairs. An ascetic and modest man, he was arrested by the Soviets in 1947, sentenced to a ten-year prison term and died in Vladimir prison in Russia. Several fellow inmates who miraculously survived the prison tortures, testified to Archbishop Reinys' saintly personality. He is a martyr for his country and his faith.[12]

Space limitations do not allow inclusions of many other men and women of distinction and achievement. The following, however, cannot be overlooked.

Stasys Šalkauskis' (1886-1941) position was unique in the party activities. He never formally belonged to the Party but his counsel was eagerly sought by the leadership on the one hand, and freely given by him on the other. He attended many of the Central Committee meetings as invited guest or volunteer participant especially when matters of State were discussed and decided. Educated in the Eastern, as well as, the Western universities, Dr. Šalkauskis dedicated his life to the scholarly endeavors as professor and later Rector of the University of Vytautas the Great. He is considered as the foremost Lithuanian philospher, and his writings to this day influence the thoughts and ideas of generations of young Lithuanians.[13]

Rev. Simanas Šultė

Simanas Šultė (1876-1920), priest, writer, scholar (holder of three doctoral degrees). An active, sincere Christian Democrat, author of many essays on Christian Democracy and related subjects. Believer and fighter for the most radical land reform, and authority on the subject.

Central Committee members of that period: *Vytautas Bičiūnas* (artist, art teacher and writer, member of the Constituent Assembly and the First Diet), *Dr. Juozas Eretas* (member of the Diet, longtime university professor, author, journalist, volunteer officer of the Independence Wars, member of the Lithuanian Catholic Academy of Sciences, organizer of athletic organizations, one of the greatest youth leaders);[14] *Rev. Juozas Dagilis* (member of the Second and Third Diets); *Mrs. Magdalena Galdikienė* (educator, leader of Catholic Women organizations, writer, member of the Constituent Assembly and all three Diets); *Vladas Jurgutis* (statesman, economist, member of the Constituent Assembly, Minister of foreign affairs, Governor of the Bank of Lithuania, longtime professor of public finance, author); *Canon Juozas Meškauskas* (professor, longtime armed forces Chaplain, judge of ecclesiastical court); *Bishop Kazimieras Paltarokas* (scholar, teacher, member of the Lithuanian Catholic Academy of Sciences, author, organizer, one of the greatest religious and national leaders under the Soviet occupation after World War II); *Dr. Klemensas Ruginis* (teacher, educational executive, editor); *Dr. Juozas Sakalauskas* (teacher, law lecturer, member of the Diet, Officer of the Foreign Ministry); *Rev. Jonas Steponavičius* (member of the Constituent Assembly and all other Diets, teacher); *Rev. Antanas Šmulkštys* (member of the Constituent Assembly and all other Diets, poet, writer); *Edvardas Turauskas* (diplomat, civic leader, journalist, member of the Diets of 1926 and 1934); *Pranas Vainauskas* (volunteer officer of Lithuanian Independence Wars, executive in the Agriculture and Finance Ministries, Minister of Commerce in the Provisional Government of 1941, Chairman of the Lithuanian Christian Democratic Union Central Committee 1949-1958, member of the Executive Committee of the Christian Democratic Union of Central Europe, 1951 to present), and others mentioned elswhere in this book.[15]

These are but a few men whose contributions to Lithuanian Christian Democracy and the Republic are outstanding. Many more share the achievements and accomplishments upon which the younger generation built a lasting basis of a Christian and democratic country. Some of them in later years carved out new careers in various fields of endeavor. Indeed later on Christian Democracy itself was hindered by many obstacles but these men and thousands of others made Christian Democracy a

Dr. Petras Karvelis

living, creative force which to this day inspires yet another generation of fellow Christian Democrats whose sad task is again to wage a struggle for freedom and liberty in and for their country.

PART VI

FOR MAN AND COUNTRY:
A STRUGGLE RENEWED

17

ON THE SIDELINES

The campaign for the Third Diet was the hottest yet. On the one hand, the Christian Democrats, after six years in power, were vulnerable as the position party always is. On the other hand, the leftists were determined to win. The opposition unmercifully clobbered the Christian Democrats for unfulfilled promises and errors, etc. At the same time, they promised the electorate anything and everything. At times, both camps embraced arguments far below their usual responsible plateau.

After three days of balloting (May 8-10, 1926), the Christian Democrats found themselves out of power. Out of 85 representatives, the party managed to elect only 30. The Populists, who gained the most, now had 22 seats, the Social Democrats — 15. For the first time, the Nationalists squeezed by with three representatives and the Farmers Party with two.[1] Also, for the first time, the Klaipėda (Memel) region had six seats.

The leftist block did not waste time in taking over. On June 7th the Diet elected Dr. K. Grinius as President and a week later, M. Sleževičius organized a new leftist cabinet.[2] Contrary to previous cabinets, there was not a single representative of the Christian Democratic block in it. The leftists meant to go it alone. The old and fruitful Christian Democratic-Populist Coalition was not revived.

There is no question that the new leftist coalition had the best intentions as far as the country's progress was concerned. The question was, and still is, were their methods and means right for the moment? Several problems became the seatbed of ever-growing discontent. The young Republic was still in transition, uneasy, and jittery. Communist elements did their utmost to undermine the nation's democratic progress. The Polish minority similarly sought every kind of privilege, not the least interested in the Republic's welfare. Neither was the rising German minority, especially in the Klaipėda region.

Under Christian Democratic rule, the government held tight reigns on these activities. A partial martial law existed, and it was a constant irritant to the leftists, especially the Social Democrats. Now in power, the Populists and Socialists not only refused to organize a coalition government with the Christian Democrats but instead, brought the minorities into the cabinet, and immediately set course for broad reforms. The martial law was lifted and the minorities' privileges increased. On top of that, the government introduced bills to reduce (if not altogether disband) the armed forces, to curtail the activities of the Catholic Theological-Philosophical Department of the State University (another irritant to the leftists), and cut off the established relationship between the State and the Church, especially in the educational field. The Chris-

Archbishop Mečislovas Reinys

tian Democrats still feeling the sting of the lost election could not and did not take all this in stride. The debates in the Diet were long and heated. Charges and counter-charges were an everyday occurrence. It was democracy at its best in theory, but not very productive in practice. Several Communist-inspired demonstrations and similar actions made the matters only worse. Of no help were some of the Social Democrats whose pronouncements were tinged with a great deal of "pink" sympathies.[3]

Contemporary historians and political analysts are debating, to this day, the legality and the political wisdom of what happened next, but on the night of December 17, 1926, a coup d'etat took place, carried out mostly by young army officers.[4] Accosted with the fait accompli, President Grinius was forced to tender his resignation as did the Prime Minister and the Cabinet. In one of his last acts, he appointed A. Voldemaras, a Nationalist, as Prime Minister. On December 19, 1926 the Diet elected A. Stulginskis as chairman and A. Smetona to be the new President of the Republic. (The new cabinet boasted two Christian Democrats, although the party's leadership did not participate in the coup d'etat. True, there was some elation about the changed course and few party members of lesser rank participated.) Formally, the bloodless coup d'etat and the change of government had all the dressings of legality.[5] The Diet was still in session and the ensuing debates were fierce. All things being equal, the coup could still have been salvaged and democracy sustained. But democracy was not the first concern of the new rulers — the Nationalist Alliance. On April 12, 1927 the new President declared the Diet dissolved and promised to announce new elections in the near future.[6] The promise was never fulfilled. Only days later, both Christian Democrats resigned from the cabinet. Thus, parliamentary democracy was ended. There were several reasons for that. Surely the new coalition of leftists (although the Populists were gravitating to center more then to the left) created conditions which breed anxiety and insecurity. Some guilt must be also attached to the system itself. Parliamentary democracy, with most of the power invested in the legislature, had a tendency to stiffle the executive and impede action. (It is of note that democracy declined at that time in almost all newly independent countries of Central Europe). Finally, to a great degree, democracy lost because its foes cherished power more than anything. This was also the case of A. Smetona and the Natonialist Alliance. The man himself was a true and even great fighter for Lithuanian independence. But his politics and his party just did not have what it takes to sway the electorate. The Nationalists in the first three elections did not win even a single seat in the Diet. Three seats in the Third Diet, surely did not promise anything. But, the temptation was always there and it was satisfied through the politically unsophisticated young officer corps.

It is not easy to define or classify the Nationalist regime which was in power for more than a decade. The most common one word definition used is authoritarianism.[7] The system had little to do with democracy but neither was it a dictatorship as practiced by Stalin or Hitler. Opposition was outlawed but it was not all-encompassing. A spoils system was definitely in action but many active Christian Democrats, Populists, and Social Democrats held important positions in various fields, even in the Ministries. It must be noted, however, that this semi-dictatorship was quite mild not only because the rulers necessarily liked it but also because the democratic strength was too great to be provoked into hostile action.

The Nationalists' political philosophy similarly escapes easy understanding. Democracy was deemed unproductive and too unpredictable. Parties in democracy were said to waste too much time and energy on selfish pursuits instead of serving the nation. Discipline and organization were stressed. (The dislike of political parties, which were finally outlawed in 1935, was such that the Nationalists called their organization an Alliance instead of a party.) President Smetona and the Nationalists tried hard to formulate a comprehensive system of ideas suited to their tastes but failed. Instead of a well thought-out creed, all they managed to produce was a very general outline of guidelines.[8]

In the meantime, the pressure from the opposition never ceased. Democracy in Lithuania was never really extinguished and even in the shadows, it held firm. So did the Christian Democrats. Their legacy spawned many new ideas and manifested itself in various creative achievements although not in state affairs or in the political field

By 1938, not only the international situation began to deteriorate, but also the Nationalist power. Their ideas just did not catch the imagination of a sophisticated intelligencia or progressive farmers. When on March 22, 1939, Nazi Germany occupied Klaipėda (Memel) region, the Nationalists realized the beginning of the end. (Sadly, the whole country realized the beginning of the end of its independence.) The Christian Democrats and the Populists surged forward in a two-pronged attack. First, they tried to rally the whole country into a unifying posture, and, secondly, both demanded from the shaken rulers re-establishment of a broad democratic basis. The Nationalists capitulated and, in a Cabinet re-shuffle, both national parties were represented. The events, however, by-passed the activities of Lithuanian political life. An immense storm was gathering in Europe and while the blood-thirsty tyrants were dividing the Continent, the Western Democracies displayed their own weaknesses for which they later paid in blood. In the rage of the tyrannical storm, Lithuania's independence again perished.

18

UNDER THE YOKE
OF TYRANNY

Just before the Soviet occupation, Lithuanian Christian Democrats gathered in conference in Kaunas. Presided by Father Mykolas Krupavičius, with the former President, A. Stulginskis, as second in command, the conference tried to assess the external and internal situation. Several hundred of younger generation Christian Democrats presented a promising picture. The intervening years on the political sidelines did not diminish either the spirit or the political acumen.[1] However, the future was more then bleak and soon it devoured all hopes. Events unfolded rapidly.

The seeds of the Lithuanian demise were sown in the secret protocols of the Non-Aggression Treaty between Communist Russia and Nazi Germany, signed on August 23, 1939. The first protocol stipulated that:

Dr. Stasys Šalkauskis

"In the event of a territorial and political re-
arrangement in the area belonging to the Baltic
States (Finland, Estonia, Latvia, and Lithuania),
the Northern boundary of Lithuania shall represent the boundary of the spheres of influence
of Germany and the USSR. In this connection,
the interests of Lithuania in the Vilna area is
recognized by each party".[2]

Only a month later, the two tyrants in yet another
secret clause (dated September 28, 1939) agreed that the
previous agreement shall be amended:

"... to the effect that the territory of the Lithuanian State falls to the sphere of influence of
the USSR".[3]

The protocol further stipulated that USSR will soon take
special measures to protect its interests in Lithuanian territory. It did just that.

After the so-called Mutual Assistance Treaty with
Lithuania was signed on October 10, 1939,[4] the Kremlin
immediately imposed military bases. It was the first step.
After Allied collapse and the fall of Paris the Kremlin,
on June 15, 1940, invaded Lithuania in force. The Soviets,
of course, tried to shroud their invasion into a seemingly
legal cloak. So-called negotiations between the two governments were held on several occasions. It was really a political and diplomatic farse. The simple fact is that Lithuania
(as well as the other two Baltic countries Latvia and
Estonia), were occupied by the force of the Red Army.[5]
The tragedy unfolded fast with all the "legal" trimmings
observed.

Dr. Juozas Eretas

To preserve the pretense, Kremlin's emmissar, V. G. Dekanozov and USSR envoy to Lithuania, Pozdniakov, arrived in Lithuania on June 15, 1940. That same day, President Smetona left the country, and the Red Army entered Lithuanian territory. Since a functioning government was necessary for "legality's" sake, Dekanozov, by force, induced the earlier resigned Prime Minister (who by the new 1938 constitution in the absence of the President was acting Chief of State) to appoint a new Prime Minister, a non-entity by the name of J. Paleckis, a communist newspaperman. Soon the new Prime Minister became President of the Republic. On June 19th several communists held in jail were released. Public meetings were held where communist speakers demanded creation of workers' "paradise". (It is of note that during the previous twenty years, Lithuanian communists never exceeded more then several hundred, and of those, the majority was composed of Lithuanian minority groups.) The same day, the Lithuanian Nationalist Alliance was outlawed. On June 25th the Lithuanian Communist Party was legalized. On June 28th the Young Communist League was legalized. On July 1st the Diet was dissolved. On July 2nd the Lithuanian Armed Forces were renamed Lithuanian Peoples Army and political commissars were introduced. On July 5th the elections to the Lithuanian People's Diet were announced. On July 14th the "elections" were held. On July 21st the new People's Diet issued two proclamations: one, announcing the creation of the Lithuanian Soviet Socialist Republic and, second, asking the Soviet Union for incorporation of the Republic into the Union. On August 3rd the Russians "accepted" L.S.S.R.'s bidding.[6]

One of the uncounted barracks in the numerous slave labor camps in the Soviet Union. Hundreds of thousands of Lithuanians perished in those camps.

In the meantime, the Lithuanian society and the whole national fabric was torn to shreds. Nightly arrests, begun the very first night, continued. All newspapers were closed. Factories and farms nationalized, organizations outlawed. Within a year, Lithuania was robbed and raped as never in its history.

The resistance against the Soviets started almost immediately and spontaneously. It was especially marked by active participation of the younger generation. It took various forms. Secret organizations sprouted everywhere. Pamphlets by the thousands were circulating not only throughout the country in general, but among high school students and the youth in particular. (University students were the most active in this movement.) Political gatherings were boycotted. Several clandestine periodicals appeared. A whole new "sub-literature" — a body of anti-communist folklore — was developed and had a tremendous impact upon the suffering population.[7]

On November 17, 1940, in Berlin, the Lithuanian Activist Front (LAF) was organized. Its main purpose was to unify all the resistance forces into a military-political network to provide leadership for anti-Soviet activities, and to prepare plans for a general uprising. (Political leadership never doubted an armed conflict between Nazi Germany and Communist Russia and deemed such a war an appropriate time to rise up against the Russian oppressors.) Although Lithuania was sealed off from the outside world, the LAF leaders kept in contact with the leadership within the country by various clandestine means.[8]

On June 15, 1941, the Soviets climaxed their terror campaign by a wave of new arrests and deportations. Over 35,000 Lithuanian citizens of all levels were herded into cattle cars and deported to Siberian slave labor camps, some located near the Arctic Ocean. Among the deportees were rich as well as poor, leaders as well as laborers, women, children, old people, sick ones, and even pregnant mothers. Hundreds died within a few days from the inhuman conditions in the cattle cars. Most of them have since perished in the Siberian wastes. Also among them were a select group of national leaders beginning with the former President of the Republic. Many other Christian Democrats of every strata within the party were among the deportees. The Soviets made sure that these men and women would never again lead the country to its freedom and independence. They also could not forgive them for actively participating in the resistance movement. (Captured documents indicated that the Soviets planned to deport ca. 700,000 Lithuanians to Russian provinces.)

No less horrendous crimes were perpetrated by the Soviets during their retreat from Lithuania at the beginning of the Russo-German War. At Petrašiūnai, Rainiai Forest, in Panevėžys and several other locations, the Red Army murdered hundreds of political prisoners and other citizens. Most of them were killed after unspeakable tortures defying comprehension.

The start of the Russo-German War on June 22, 1941, signaled also the start of the LAF planned insurrection, which was executed in a most expeditious and highly successful manner. Within a few days, Lithuanians rid themselves of the Red Army with little help from the invading Germans. (As a matter of fact, many a town greeted the Germans as a free Lithuanian town — the Soviets were already driven out. This was, of course, never acknowledged by Nazi Germany.) Needless to say, the insurrection had the support of every Lithuanian. Many an untrained youngster joined the pitched battles against the hated oppressors. Two thousand men fell in combat.[9]

Already on June 23, 1941 the LAF announced the Formation of the Provisional Government with LAF leader, Colonel K. Škirpa, as Prime Minister. However, the Germans had other plans. After severely reprimanding the Berlin-based Prime Minister for his actions, they never allowed him to return to his country. Thus, for the next six weeks (the life of the government), the Cabinet was presided by the Minister of Education, J. Ambrazevičius.

The Provisional Government was never part of the German plans. Only its immense popularity in the country, and the knowledge by the international community of its existence, saved it from an early annihilation. Even then, the Germans permitted it to function for only six weeks. No less imperialistic than Stalin's Russia, Hitler's Germany had different notions about Lithuanian independence. The government accomplished a great deal. The cabinet courage was great in the face of the almighty German power. However, after brave attempts to come to some honorable agreement with the new oppressors the Cabinet was liquidated and the Germans took complete control.

Christian Democrats actively participated in the Cabinet as well as in other activities. The Cabinet boasted three Christian Democrats: *Pranas Vainauskas,* Minister of Commerce, volunteer officer of the wars of independence, member of the Central Committee and later longtime Chairman of the Lithuanian Christian Democratic Union as well as a high official of the Christian Democratic Union of Central Europe (CDUCE). *Jonas Matulionis,* Minister of Finance, also a volunteer officer of the wars of independence, longtime Central Committee member

157

Dr. Pranas Dovydaitis

and party manager, later the first President of the World Lithuanian Community and, for a time, Chairman of the Supreme Committee for Liberation of Lithuania. *Balys Vitkus* Minister of Agriculture, one of the foremost leaders of the Christian Democratic Farmers Union of Lithuania.

German designs soon became clear to all Lithuanians. Their intermediate aim was to use the country as a supplier of food-stuffs and labor force for the German war machine. The ultimate plan was to annihilate most of the indigenous population, colonize the land and annex it to Germany as a province of the Reich. This realization also gave birth to yet another resistance movement which was just as effective and active as the resistance against the Soviets. Numerous underground newspapers were in circulation. Secret groups and organizations successfully thwarted many a German plot to exploit Lithuania and its people.[10]

The Germans tried various means to exploit the economy and recruit manpower. However, their pleas fell on deaf ears of the defiant population. The oppressive Nazi might could neither recruit appreciable numbers of laborers for the war machine nor organize a separate Lithuanian SS Legion. (As a matter of fact, Lithuania was the only German occupied country which did not organize such a legion).[11]

Such defiance, of course, irritated the Nazis. Their "superhuman" philosophy was no less destructive then the "proletariat dictatorship" of the Soviets. Thousands of Lithuanian citizens of Jewish faith were exterminated forthwith. Only a few hundred escaped the beastly extermination plot, mostly aided by their fellow citizens. There are as yet uncounted instances of valor on the part of Lithuanians who bravely tried to save as many lives of

Mrs. Magdalena Galdikienė

their Jewish fellow citizens as possible, but the Nazi machine was too swift and too well oiled.

One of the first victims was none other than Mykolas Krupavičius. As related before, he barely escaped deportation by the Soviets. After the German occupation, with the Provisional Government destroyed, he took it upon himself as a former member of the Diet and the government, to counter the devious Nazi actions. In three lenghty memoranda addressed to the Commissioner General of Lithuania (the highest Nazi overlord of the country), he bravely and candidly explored German designs against the nation. The memoranda deplored the whole policy of the German government towards Lithuania and in no uncertain terms demanded the end of the murder of Jews, the colonization by Germans, and the persecution of the Poles.

The third memorandum was also signed by two other national figures: former President Dr. Kazys Grinius, and former Minister of Agriculture, Jonas Aleksa.[12] German reaction was swift. On December 5, 1942, Mykolas Krupavičius and Jonas Aleksa were imprisoned and deported to Germany. President Grinius, because of ill health, was kept under house arrest in his native village. Father Krupavičius, after a spell in German prisons, was later put under house arrest in Germany until the end of the War.[13]

These political prisoners were soon followed by many others. Notable among them was a group of 46 intellectuals arrested on March 16-17, 1943, and shipped off to the infamous Stuthoff concentration camp. Several of this group died there as martyrs for liberty and freedom. Some were captured by the Soviets and again incarcerated. Some managed to survive both, and reached the Free World.

161

Dr. Antanas Trimakas

One of the lasting achievements of the universal resistance against the Nazis was the unification of the national effort under one leadership. Up to the middle of 1943, numerous organizations and groups fought the unequal battles against the oppressors. During the second half of that year, the overall leadership had been concentrated in two committees: Supreme Lithuanian Committee which embraced all the leftist groups, and the Council of Lithuania which united the groups of Catholic persuasion. Exercising a great deal of political acumen and statesmanship, these two authorities soon merged. On November 25, 1943 the new and all-embracing Supreme Committee for Liberation of Lithuania held its first meeting.[14] On February 16, 1944 (Lithuanian Independence Day) the Committee published a declaration "To the Lithuanian Nation". It said in part that:

> "The sovereign state of Lithuania did not disappear either because of the Soviet or because of the present occupation by the Reich, only the functioning of the organs of the sovereign state had been temporarily interrupted. This functioning interrupted by the Soviet Union occupation on June 15, 1940 and by acts committed by force and fraud under the violent pressures of this occupation was temporarily restored by the National Insurrection of June 23, 1941 and by activities of the Provisional Government".[15]

The Supreme Committee had the trust of the whole nation. It is still functioning and is regarded by Lithuanians as the highest political institution in exile.[16]

163

The third act of the Lithuanian Drama of Oppression began in the Fall of 1944 when the Red Army reconquered Lithuanian territory. It is well beyond the scope of this paper to attempt even an outline of the past 25 years of Soviet domination in Lithuania. It will suffice to say that there are few examples in modern history of a more cruel and beastly exploitation of a nation. Two main points illustrate the whole tragedy and its scope.

On the one hand, the Soviets, to this day, are following the policy of genocide. Their ultimate goal is nothing less then the extermination of the whole Lithuanian population. It is not the first people to be earmarked for such ignominious end. The Soviets have already exterminated several national groups in the past. All the Soviet actions in every field of endeavor in occupied Lithuania emanate from this master policy. Since 1949, the Soviets have exterminated more than 700,000 Lithuanian nationals. This genocide slowly but surely continues to this day. It is the overriding fact in Lithuanian problematics.[17]

On the other hand, the nation waged a collosal struggle against this Soviet predetermined destiny. For eight years, (1944-1952) Lithuanian guerillas, one hundred thousand strong and completely dedicated, organized and armed, waged a courageous battle against the Kremlin tyranny. According to Soviet-own documents, the partisans for several years took charge of much of the countryside. They commanded the loyalty of the great majority of the population and inflicted severe damage to the Red Army. Most of them sacrificed their lives for their country and although they did not prevail, they left an immense legacy of honor to future generations. They reinforced the spirit of resistance within the country as well as without.[18]

164

It is gratifying to note that, in general, the Western powers do not recognize de jure the present Lithuanian situation. Shortly after the fake elections to the so-called "People's Diet", the Acting Secretary of State of the United States Sumner Welles issued a statement which said in part:

> "During these past few days, the devious processes whereunder the political independence and territorial integrity of the three Baltic Republics — Estonia, Latvia, and Lithuania — were to be deliberately annihilated by one of their more powerful neighbors, have been rapidly drawing to their conclusion... The people of the United States are opposed to predatory activities no matter whether they are carried on by the use of force or by the threat of force... The United States will continue to stand by these principles..."[19]

The stand of Great Britain was clearly stated by Winston Churchill:

> "We have never recognized the 1941 frontiers of Russia... They were acquired by acts of aggression in shameful collusion with Hitler...[20] The Baltic States should be sovereign independent peoples..."[21]

France, Germany, Italy, and most of the South American States follow a similar pattern of non-recognition

165

as does Canada, and some other members of the British Commonwealth. The consensus of international community is that Lithuania's international personality is intact and that the annexation is unlawful and illegal.[22]

This then is the great equasion of Lithuania's future: genocide against the total commitment for freedom and independence. It is a struggle not unlike that of David and Goliath. And the fight is not yet over.[23]

LCDU Central Committee in the early fifties. L. to r. Chairman Pranas Vainauskas, Msgr. Mykolas Krupavičius, Stasys Lušys. Second row: Albinas Gražiūnas, Antanas Bendorius, Dr. Vladas Viliamas.

19

IN POLITICAL EXILE

When the ravages of the second World War ended, Lithuanian Christian Democrats were scattered all over the world. Some of the foremost leaders and thousands of members of the Party were massacred or imprisoned by the Soviets in Siberian slave labor camps. The great majority were again under the yoke of tyranny. A relatively small group of leaders and members found themselves homeless, in exile, scattered through several Western European countries. To this group fell the responsibility of carrying on the struggle for the Homeland as well as the work of Christian Democracy. The Republic was no more. The Lithuanian soil was no more. Hope was dim. And yet, the responsibility and the work was immense.

The majority of Christian Democrats, as well as, most of Lithuania's exiles, found themselves in war-ravaged Germany living in Displaced Persons Camps aided by the Allies and the United Nations. For several years,

167

Several delegates of the LCDU conference in New York in 1954. Seated from left: the than Chairman of the Central Committee Pranas Vainauskas, Msgr. M. Krupavičius, Dr. K. Pakštas, Msgr. J. Balkūnas, Canon J. Meškauskas.

all energies were expanded to survival and the common struggle for liberation. It was inconceivable to them that the victorious Western Powers would be so duped as to permit the Soviet Union to dominate not only Eastern and Central Europe, but to a great degree, the world affairs. By the late Forties, however, it was clear to all that the Free World was indeed on a different course.

At that time, Christian Democrats began organizing again. In a conference in Stuttgart, Germany, the exiles united their efforts into the Lithuanian Christian Democratic Union with Mykolas Krupavičius as Chairman.

During 1949-1950 migration, most of the Christian Democrats settled in the United States. The Union structure was re-organized and a new Central Committee elected in 1950. For four successive two-year terms, the Central Committee had its headquarters in New York and was headed by *Pranas Vainauskas,* a longtime Party leader and former Minister of Commerce in the Provisional Government. For the next six years, the Union was directed by a Chicago-based Central Committee chaired by *Dr. Kazys Šidlauskas,* a Harvard lawyer and a leader of the younger generation. During 1964-1973 the Central Committee resided in Cleveland and was headed by *Algirdas J. Kasulaitis.* Presently the Central Committee is again in Chicago, headed by *Vladas Šoliūnas.* Sizable chapters of the Union are active in New York, Chicago, Cleveland, Boston, Detroit, Toronto, Canada, and other North American cities. Smaller groups of Christian Democrats are active in Australia, Germany, Italy, France, Brazil, etc. European members of the Union are headed by Lithuanian Christian Democratic Council of Europe presided by *Adolfas Venskus,* one of the most outstanding leaders of the younger generation.

For a time, Christian Democratic Youth activities were centered in Christian Democratic Study Clubs, mostly in the United States and Canada. Political education through lectures and study groups, discussions and panel shows were their main activity. Political, economic, social, and other subjects were studied, evaluated, and put to practical test wherever and however possible. The Study Clubs also published their own review *"Jaunimo Žygiai"* (The Deeds of Youth) which enjoyed a sizable influence among Lithuanian youth. Presently, the youth activities are integrated into the larger framework within the Union.

Participants in the 1969 LCDU leadership conference in Cleveland, Ohio, USA. Seated l. to r.: Stasys Alšėnas, Julius Staniškis, Petras Kliorys, the then Chairman of the Central Committee Dr. Kazys Šidlauskas, Msgr. Mykolas Krupavičius, immediate pastChairman Pranas Vainauskas, Dr. Vladas Litas. Standing from the left: Petras Tamulionis, Lionginas Leknickas, Petras Balčiūnas, Petras Maldeikis, Algirdas J. Kasulaitis, Dr. Jurgis Balčiūnas, Pranas Povilaitis, Petras Stravinskas, Petras Žilinskas and Petras Gruodis.

Although organized activities of the Union are hinder-ed primarily by the dispersal of its membership throughout the world, Lithuanian Christian Democrats are active in many fields within the sizable exile community.

The Lithuanian Christian Democratic Union pursues several well defined courses of action. The greatest share of all labors, of course, is dedicated to the single cause of all Lithuanians — the struggle for freedom and inde-pendence. Christian Democratic representatives actively participate in various specific organizations dedicated to direct liberation work, as well as, to many other groups which indirectly participate in those activities. In many cases, the Christian Democrats are in leadership positions. Most of Lithuanian Christian Democratic Union's action in this field is concentrated in and channeled through the Supreme Committee for Liberation of Lithuania which, as mentioned previously, is the highest Lithuanian politi-cal authority in charge of all liberation activities. The Committee presently embraces all Lithuanian political groups and other specific organizations — 15 in all. In this all-encompassing unity lies the Committee's strength and authority. The Christian Democrats participated in the Committee since its inception during the German oc-cupation in 1943, and aided its work in a most substantial way. Consequently, from the very beginning, the Christian Democrats played key roles in the Committee. In 1944-1954 the Committee was headed by Mykolas Krupavičius. He was succeeded by *Jonas Matulionis* who in turn was replaced by one of the leaders of the Christian Democratic Farmers Union, *Dr. Antanas Trimakas.* After two years of Chairmanship by a representative of the Farmers Party *Vaclovas Sidzikauskas,* the Committee again elected a member of the Farmers Union, *Dr. Kęstutis J. Valiūnas* to head the Executive Council as Chairman. This almost uninterrupted responsibility and trust puts a substantial burden on the Union's resources and capabilities, which are carried out with utmost diligence and concern.

The Union is also active in the international field. On the one hand, it endeavors to participate in the great thrust forward experienced by the international community of Christian Democracy. On the other hand, it is in constant viligance trying to gather anti-communist forces, as well as, aid the cause of Lithuania's independence struggle. Lithuanian Christian Democratic Union belongs to the *European Union of Christian Democrats* and to the *Christian Democratic Union of Central Europe*. The latter international organization was actually established by the efforts of one of the most prominent leaders of Christian Democracy — *Dr. Kazys Pakštas*, who for a while, was also one of the Vice-Chairmen of the Council of CDUCE. Dr. Pakštas (1893-1960) was a most extraordinary man. An internationally recognized scholar, a master of eight languages, a specialist in geopolitics, a hypnotizing lecturer, and one of the shrewdest political analysts, Dr. Pakštas was also an apostle of federalism — primarily the Central European type.[1] This concept brought him to the idea of CDUCE of which he was one of the key architects.

To aid in this endeavor, Lithuanian Christian Democratic Union has representatives in several key cities: Paris, Rome, Rio de Janeiro, Basel, Baden-Baden, Montevideo, etc. At the same time, it has its representatives in major international centers of Christian Democracy. Youth is also represented in international bodies and various gatherings.

172

Dr. Kazys Pakštas

Individual Christian Democrats are active in various fields of endeavor in general. (Lithuanian cultural and civic life is quite active in the United States and a score of other countries.) Mykolas Krupavičius is the author of the *Lithuanian Charter*, a body of postulates which guides the thousands of Lithuanians in their exile labors. He is also the Father of World Lithuanian Community, an institution which embraces Lithuanian exiles and emigrees throughout the world. The first president of the community was also a Christian Democrat, the before mentioned Jonas Matulionis. *Leonardas Šimutis,* a member of he Third Diet and later the foremost leader of Lithuanian-American Community, for twenty-five years was also the President of Lithuanian American Council, the main political action organization of Lithuanians in the United States.[2] Many other Christian Democrats are contributing substantially to the overall cultural and civic life of Lithuanian communities in various fields and countries.

Lithuanian Christian Democratic Union also publishes the respected political and social review *"Tėvynės Sargas"* (The Guardian of Homeland) and Lithuanian Christian Democratic Bulletin (both in Lithuanian).

These activities are an outgrowth of several basic goals thrust upon Lithuanian Christian Democracy in exile.

First and foremost, of course, is the struggle for freedom and independence. No Lithuanian will ever accept the sometimes implied notion that the Lithuanian problem is not relevant, especially in the context of supposedly larger international picture. Power politics and pragmatic philosophy cannot change the fact that every nation has the inalienable right to self-determination, freedom

174

Pranas Vainauskas

and independence. This right applies not only to the super-powers but to small countries as well. It is not a privilege granted by some cynical superpower but an inherent right. To deny this right to one country is to deny the basic precepts of democracy itself.

No less important a goal is aiding the enslaved na-tions in every way possible. It is an established fact that genocidal policies are in effect in occupied Lithuania to-day, as they were from the very beginning of oppression. Realistic analysis presents rather depressing conclusions. Lithuania is being exterminated physically and dissolved spiritually. It is literally in the throws of death. This fact is a most compelling imperative for action.

Third, exile conditions are not very condusive for either cultural growth or preservation of national con-sciousness. Thusly, the concerted effort to create an envi-ronment and an atmosphere where the Lithuanian way of life could flourish until the time when the nation, free again, could once more assert itself and continue the in-terrupted creative progress. Lithuania is a small part of the international society and, in another sense, of total humanity, but it has the right and the potential to con-tribute to human affairs its own share of values. This share might be small but it is unique. To presume that only the large and powerful nations have the capacity to add to the collective endeavors of humanity is to ignore historical experience.[3]

Fourth, Lithuanian Christian Democrats perceive Christian Democracy as a living and growing ideal. It must, therefore, be nurtured by new thoughts, new ideas, and new applications. Study, analysis, and experiences are the tools which continuously improve the Christian De-mocratic system, its methods, and its application.

176

Finally, the Christian Democrats strongly believe that federated Europe presents the best possibilities for every European country in terms of security, economic development, and cultural growth. Consequently, they endeavor to promote such a federal idea and create a favorable climate for it among the exiles, as well as, among all Europeans by all means and channels available to them.

This forward look is keeping the Lithuanian Christian Democratic Union alive, energetic, and a progressive movement, dedicated to the high principles of Christian Democracy and sure of purpose in its struggle for national freedom and independence.

LCDU Central Committee of the mid-sixties. L. to r. Pranas Razgaitis, Petras Balčiūnas, Stasys Lušys, Antanas Tamulionis, Petras Kliorys, Chairman Algirdas J. Kasulaitis, Dr. Kazys Šidlauskas, Pranas Vainauskas and Henrikas Idzelis.

20

CHRISTIAN DEMOCRACY
CHALLENGED

As a social and political ideal, Christian Democracy is challenged in terms of its precepts by the pluralistic world society. It is only natural since the majority of the members are not Christians in the first place. A much more direct and down to earth challenge is posed in several countries where Christian Democracy is a part of the general social and political structure, especially where it is in a position to exert influence and determine the social and political course. However, as a truly international movement, Christian Democracy is challenged on still another plane, namely in terms of its principles in relation to the international situation.

It is not the intent of this short chapter to analyze or even outline the first two challenges. The first challenge is in the realm of political and social philosophy and ideology, and merits in-depth study on its own. (As a matter of fact, there is already a body of literature on the subject.) The second challenge is similarly too wide in scope and too varied in its several national applications to take up here. However, the third challenge has relevancy not only in itself, but also in terms of the subject matter of this paper. As a national movement limited to a body politic, it has international responsibilities only in terms of its position within the power structure of that body politic. (This would be applicable only to Christian Democratic governments.) However, as a universal body of social and political thought and an international political movement, Christian Democracy cannot escape international responsibilities.[1] It cannot limit its interests within parochial boundaries without compromising its basic tenets which are the core of its very relevancy. Thus, the question what is Christian Democracy's responsibilities towards Lithuania and other enslaved nations, as well as towards freedom, liberty, and independence in general? The answer to this question as well as the action based on this answer, constitutes the very challenge mentioned above. The Lithuanian situation serves as a guide to this challenge and how Christian Democracy is responding to it.

The situation creating this challenge is quite clear. Lithuania and other enslaved nations are being exploited, degraded, and exterminated. All international laws and covenants have been, and are being, broken every day. The Soviet Union is perpetrating all sorts of crimes including the dreaded genocide. This is one side of the equasion. On the other side, is the Free World's Christian Democracy. Its basic tenets are justice, peace, law, order,

179

Dr. Kazys Šidlauskas

and love. It exists in free societies, unhindered by persecution, punishment, or forcible adverse influences. It is in position to freely think, create, and act. It can speak out or keep quiet. How it responds to this challenge is immensely important. For the response indicates if Christian Democracy is a live, true, and responsible idea, capable of creating order out of chaos, well-being out of poverty, peace out of violence, or is it only another political slogan directed to seeking power, privileges and the good life for a few.

Admittedly, the several national Christian Democracies face many more challenges. It would be unfair to expect that every Christian Democrat should dedicate all his energies in the international field. Christianity itself teaches man to love his neighbor, and that primarily means his family, his fellow citizens, his country, etc. in that order. It is natural and no one really questions neither the priorities nor the ethics behind them. But, Christian Democracy is an idea that supersedes political boundaries. Its strength lies, to a great degree, in its all-embracing universal principles which cannot be limited to a group, a class, or even a country. It is always national only in part. It must always be universal in its striving for a better world. It cannot enjoy freedom without sharing it. It cannot realize justice without struggling for justice for all. It cannot embrace freedom without dedicating its energies to fighting for it for the benefit of all. This is the great imperative which should play a key role in the beforementioned equasion.

Christian Democracy cannot close its eyes and its heart to the suffering of others. Millions of people in a score of countries which are terrorized by the modern imperialism of the Soviet Union. It cannot maintain that

181

the struggle for freedom and liberty is not its business. It cannot fall back on its priorities, legitimate as they are, to justify disinterest in the wider world community. It must share its blessings with those who are less fortunate. It must speak out for those who are silenced. It must aid those who are in need of help. It must live up to its ideal. There is no more a dangerous course for Christian Democracy then the one which will narrow its horizons and envelope its thrust within selfish boundaries.

It would serve no purpose in this context to analyze who did what, when, and how. Neither is it necessary to map actions which would benefit the enslaved nations and millions of suffering people. Every national party, every international union, indeed every individual Christian Democrat must analyze past performances and future for itself. Just as those millions of people cannot, at this time, escape the shackles of their destiny, so Christian Democracy cannot escape its responsibility towards those suffering millions of fellow human beings. There are many ways and means to join the struggle of the enslaved nations. The exile Christian Democratic brethren need help —a voice to inform, print to enlighten, recognition to sustain hope, and other resources to continue the fight. It matters less who, when, and how much each Christian Democrat gives. It is much more important that every one realizes the inescapable moral obligation to his fellowman. One hundred million people of the captive nations are at stake. At the same time, the very relevancy of Christian Democracy is at the crossroads. To do too much is not necessary; to do less is to surrender the bright future of a great ideal to the momentary benefit of the ever-changing present.

182

Members of the presents (1975) Central Committee of L.C.D.U.: (left to right) Juozas Paškus; Adomas Viliušis; Stasys Liūšys; Dr. Aldona Rugis; Vladas Šoliū-nas, pres.; Pranas Povilaitis.

Status quo is always a temptation when self-interest is served. Some Christian Democracies are in a position to embrace such momentary tranquility, and close their eyes to the turmoil and violence outside their borders. However, turmoil and violence supersedes political boundaries just as Christian Democracy does. A decade of peace, even a year, or a day, is a precious thing, but never at the expense of others. Peace, liberty, and justice are indivisible.[2] As long as one country is enslaved, no country is truly independent. As long as one man is deprived of his basic rights, no man is really free. As long as Communism is unchecked, no nation and no man is safe. Indeed Communism is still the greatest threat not only to Democracy, but to Christianity itself.[3]

It is tragic that the Western World still does not realize the mammoth threat emanating from international Communism. Immersed in self and selfish interests, the Free World too readily embraces every little inconsequential sign of the so-called Communist change. It overjoys at every minute improvement, be it genuine or superficial. But Communism does not and cannot change. Its self proclaimed eschatological and apocalyptic mission is just as valid to Communists today as it was decades ago. It is more then just a political or social system, and therefore its aims are higher. It is a pseudo-religion, and its ultimate goal is to re-create human nature itself. Its master plan envisions man who is not a reflection of Almighty God, but a copy of a well functioning machine.[4]

It is not inconceivable that Communism might create satisfactory material conditions to satisfy man's physical needs. It is quite possible that it could cause considerable scientific and technological progress. It is even probable that peace could be achieved under universal Communist

184

rule. But for every piece of bread, a television set or a car, man will pay with his freedom. For every technological step forward, he will take a step backward in his liberty. For every day of Communist peace, man will give up his very soul.[5]

Only at the risk of its very way of life, can the Free World afford to ignore Communism and its advances. Only a suicidal urge can excuse the folly of disinterest. Only tragedy can mark the future if the present is ignored and discounted.

Communist challenge is the reality of today and not of tomorrow. It is a challenge to the very roots of Christian civilization. It is no coincidence that Communism first annihilates Christian thought and the immortal soul before it reaches for the rest of man or nation. Christianity, as the cradle of Western civilization, is the only effective force of history that not only can defeat the evil Communist ideology, but also create conditions for the human race which will be condusive to universal progress and peace. This is the reason why Christianity, according to the Communist master plan, must perish.[6] This is the reason why it is being exterminated behind the Iron Curtain. With Christianity exterminated, how long will Western civilization itself survive? This is the question that the Free World cannot afford not to ponder. But why then are only the enslaved people expected to sacrifice everything in this historic struggle? This is yet another question the Free World is not willing to answer. This very unwillingness is the ultimate challenge to Christian Democracy, as well as, to the entire Western World.

Lithuania and other enslaved countries are today a battleground of this momentous confrontation. At stake is not only the several nations with millions of people, but

185

the region's democracy and Christianity itself. In a very true sense, its struggle is everyone's struggle.[7] Lithuanians on both sides of the Iron Curtain are carrying their share of the battle. What share is being carried by the international community of Christian Democracy and the Free World in general is a question which only they can answer. But answer they must. If not today, then tomorrow because wishful thinking will not cause Communism to disappear. Lithuanian Christian Democrats took up the challenge a long time ago. They will persevere. In unity with their brethren of all nations, alone if need be. For free men, this noble struggle for liberty and justice is the only way to live.

Appendices

SELECTED DOCUMENTS

THE MEMBERS OF THE UNION OF LITH-UNIAN CHRISTIAN DEMOCRATS, DIS-LODGED FROM THEIR NATIVE LAND BY THE SOVIET OCCUPATION AND ASSEM-BLED IN CONFERENCE IN NEW YORK, ON MAY 29 AND 30, 1954, TO COMMERATE THE CENTENNIAL ANNIVERSARY OF THE INITIAL MANIFESTATION OF CHRISTIAN DEMOCRATIC IDEAS IN LITHUANIA, THE 64TH ANNIVERSARY OF THE FOUNDING OF THE FIRST LITHUANIAN CHRISTIAN DEMOCRATIC MINDED NEWSPAPER "THE REVIEW", AND THE 50TH ANNIVERSARY OF THE FORMULATION OF THE FIRST LITHUANIAN CHRISTIAN DEMOCRATIC PROGRAM,

solemnly make the following

DECLARATION

1. Christian Democratic ideas first appeared in Lithu-ania one hundred years ago. These ideas, moulded to fit

the local living conditions, met with wide acceptance. Later, the first formally published program of Christian Democrats clarified and crystalized the political thinking of the large Catholic Lithuanian public and enabled the masses to present a united front in the struggle for the nation's freedom.

2. With the economic, cultural, social and political program of the country based firmly on Christian Democratic principles, independent Lithuania made rapid progress in all spheres on both personal and national levels, thereby graphically proving the soundness of these principles.

3. The important achievement by the Lithuanian Christian Democrats in the years of independence — the drawing up and adoption in 1922 of Lithuania's Constitution, the agrarian reform, the workers' social security laws, the advanced educational system, the equitable treatment of national minorities — according to today's most enlightened viewpoint, national and international, were the result of deeply democratic, cultural, and liberal political theory of government.

These facts clearly indicate that Lithuania's future reconstruction, progress and welfare will again require a foundation of Christian Democratic principles. Guided by this conviction, the Lithuanian Christian Democrats feel bound by their national conscience to tighten their ranks and increase their efforts both in the fight for Lithuania's freedom and in the preparation for liberated Lithuania's reconstruction. Therefore, the Lithuanian Christian Democrats

hereby solemnly resolve:
1. To fight for Lithuania's liberation with even great-

er sacrifice and determination and to consider this a fundamental obligation.

2. With all possible strength to assist not only in preserving, but in increasing, the Lithuanian national and cultural potential as an important factor for the country's rehabilitation.

3. In the name of closer unity among the Lithuanians, and regardless of the international situation, the Supreme Committee for Liberation of Lithuania remains the chief authority in Lithuania's liberation activities this side of the Iron Curtain.

4. To study carefully the problems connected with liberated Lithuania's rehabilitation and to join with other Lithuanian institutions engaged in this work.

At the same time, the Conference of Lithuanian Christian Democrats,
    hereby appeals:

I. TO ALL LITHUANIAN CHRISTIAN DEMOCRATS THROUGHOUT THE FREE WORLD

1. To consider participation in the above-mentioned activities as an irrevocable obligation.

2. Wherever possible to join organized units of Lithuanian Christian Democrats, for the tremendous tasks require joint effort.

3. Carefully to observe the developments in political thinking in the entire free world, paying special attention to Christian Democratic concepts and their practical application, so that liberated Lithuania may have the benefit of the most advanced ideas on which to base her reconstruction.

II. TO THE CHRISTIAN LITHUANIAN PUBLIC

1. The Conference recalls that the passiveness and insufficient participation in the political field by Christians everywhere have not only brought immense harm to the Christians, but have also retarded the political, social and cultural progress in their respective countries. In these critical times such indifference can bring catastrophic results. For this reason even Pope Pius XII has urged the Catholic world that in these times participation of Catholics in political affairs is their sacred duty. Greater attention should therefore be given by the entire Christian Lithuanian public to a deeper study of political theory and organizations and to intensification of political action.

2. The Conference directs the attention to a recent trend to propagate formalistic democracy with its disregard of Christian ideals and principles. These democratic forms alone, devoid of principles and definite pursuable values, do not promote a wholesome development of a state or its people. The inherent dangers of such a doctrine ought to be recognized and every effort must be made to base the public order upon Christian teachings.

3. The tendency for even the Christian Lithuanian public to split up into numerous groups politically is a grave misfortune, which, if left uncorrected, may bring serious consequences to Christianity, the state and the people. This matter requires serious attention.

III. TO THE LITHUANIANS THROUGHOUT THE FREE WORLD

1. In view of the current world tensions, all Lithuanians living in the free world are obligated by the se-

riousness of the times to increase their efforts in the cause of Lithuania's liberation, to help keep alive all national and cultural activity and prepare for the rebuilding of Lithuania.

2. Lithuanians living in the free world are urged not only to be more vigilant and ready, but also to be more closely united, better disciplined and have a sense of responsibility relative to fulfillment and neglect of their duties, so that all would be in harmony with the great aims and national aspirations.

IV. TO OUR FIGHTING BRETHREN IN LITHUANIA

1. The Jubilee Conference of Lithuanian Christian Democrats salutes the warriors in the fatherland and expresses its deep conviction that Lithuania's hour of liberation will surely come. The suffering and the sacrifice of our brothers behind the Iron Curtain are well known. Their heroic efforts to resist all designs of the oppressor and to defend and preserve what has been sacred to the Lithuanian for centuries is followed with deep earnestness. Their noble example is a stimulus to those in the free world to labor diligently and incessantly that Lithuania may soon have its day of freedom.

2. The Conference wishes that it be known that the Lithuanians in the free world are expending great efforts for the liberation of their fatherland and that these efforts are bringing results. The liberation of Lithuania is today the hope and aim not only of Lithuanians; it has become a prime objective of the entire free world, which seeks to free all enslaved nations from the communist yoke.

192

The Lithuanians form a united front with other peoples who are fighting for their freedom. There is no power on earth that can keep these hundreds of millions of freedom-loving men in slavery for long. Though the path before the Lithuanian people is one of struggle, suffering and sacrifice, there is no basis for despair. It can be said with certainty that at the end of the road lies freedom and resurrection of the ancient land to a new life. In our difficult journey toward that happy day may God protect us all and may He shorten the travail of our fatherland.

V. TO OUR FRIENDS AND ALLIES IN THE SOVIET-ENSLAVED NATIONS

1. The Conference firmly believes that the deliverance of Soviet-enslaved peoples will come to a great extent through their own efforts. In the great expanse from the Baltic and Adriatic Seas to the Far East the enslaved nations comprise hundreds of millions of people. These millions, together with their brethren in the free world, will break the chains of bondage, if they face up to the imperialistic oppressor with unity and determination. The efforts of all these nations must be coordinated and all resources must be mobilized.

2. The Conference welcomes the measures being taken by these nations and pledges them every possible support. It takes special notice of the determination of the Eastern European nations to act in unison. This sort of unified effort plus the great and significant aid from the United States of America give credence to the belief that the subjugated lands will rise again to a life of freedom.

VI. TO THE NATIONS OF THE FREE WORLD

1. The Lithuanian Christian Democrats having experienced at first hand the communist regime, its lies, its massacres and its denial of all human and national rights, are moved to express their deepest conviction that a peaceful co-existence of the free world and the communist world is impossible. The world will not see peace until communism is finally and utterly destroyed.

2. The Conference wholeheartedly approves the resolution passed by the International Union of Christian Democrats (Nouvelles Equipes Internationales) at its 1952 congress and confirmed in 1953, and respectfully invites all free nations and every person who has respect for the rights of nations and individuals to study and support this clearly defined outline of action, which resolution stresses the following:

    a. To never exclude from their upper-most concerns the fate of the oppressed peoples.

    b. to oppose by all their energies any dealings with the oppressor based on *political bargaining* in relation to the fate of the people who are victims of communist aggression.

    c. to oppose any attempt to recognize the situation in the oppressed countries as definite, stable, or legal.

    d. to proclaim the principle of moral and penal responsibility of all those guilty of crimes against humanity in the oppressed countries.

    e. to affirm once more that Europe will not regain its serenity and political and economic balance as

194

long as the people of Central and Eastern Europe are not free.

f. to draw up plans and agreements, supported by Western Christian Democrats, for reconstruction and recovery of the oppressed countries after their liberation.

3. The Conference voices its approval of the proposed European Federation as it is being envisaged by the International Union of Christian Democrats and recently outlined by the Christian Democrats of Central Europe. The Lithuanian Christian Democrats pledge their cooperation with these and similar movements for the propagation and realization of the Federation idea.

MAY THE ALMIGHTY GOD BLESS THE EFFORTS BEING EXPENDED EVERYWHERE TO RECOVER THE RIGHTS AND FREEDOMS FOR ALL NATIONS AND INDIVIDUALS

LITHUANIAN CHRISTIAN DEMOCRAT-
IC UNION SOLEMNLY COMMEMORAT-
ING THE SEVEN HUNDRED AND
EIGHTEENTH ANNIVERSARY OF THE
CREATION OF LITHUANIAN KINGDOM,
AND THE FIFTIETH ANNIVERSARY
OF THE REESTABLISHMENT OF THE
LITHUANIAN REPUBLIC; HONORING
THE SACRED MEMORY OF THE FAL-
LEN BROTHERS, AND REAFFIRMING
ITS DETERMINATION TO CONTINUE
ITS FIGHT FOR FREEDOM AND INDE-
PENDENCE, PROCLAIMS TO LITHUA-
NIANS EVERYWHERE THE FOLLO-
WING

DECLARATION

The Fight for Freedom

The right to freedom and independence is based on
Natural Law. Every deviation from this Law is an international crime, denounced by solemn declarations and
international covenants. The Soviet Russian occupation of
Lithuania is not only a crime against the Lithuanian
Nation, but also against the Natural Law and the conscience of mankind. The enslavement of Lithuanians is
a crime against every Lithuanian, who like the whole nation, has the sacred right to live in freedom according to
the will of the Creator and the precepts of his conscience.

Therefore, every Lithuanian must be a fighter against the Soviet Union and international Communism, as well as against any and all their manifestations.

With reverance in our hearts and prayer on our lips we bow our heads to those brothers and sisters who perished in the heroic struggles for the independence of Lithuania and the freedom of every countryman. We bow our heads to those who suffered for justice and principles, for man and conscience. We bow our heads to those who even during this night of slavery hold the freedom torch high and guard its flame with their very lives.

We note with gratification that the United States and many other countries did not and do not recognize the cruel Soviet occupation of Lithuania. This non-recognition is in itself a condemnation of the Soviet Union which by that and subsequent acts, has committed a crime against the principles of law and justice, as well as against the United Nations Charter and the Universal Declaration on Human Rights.

Commemorating these grandiose anniversaries, we must again confront the realities of home and exile. Let us off-set the sorrowful exile existence by the fire of creative endeavor, which transforms the word, the thought, and the deed; let us permeate the barren present of exile by creative thrusts which pave the road to true progress.

Let us join our forces in a meaningful unity within the Supreme Committee for Liberation of Lithuania which is leading the political struggle for liberty and freedom. The Supreme Committee has the mandate to represent and act for Lithuania. Let us help to create conditions for the Committee, so that it will be able to unfold the banners of battle on all fronts. Let us open the eyes of the

197

world to the Soviet Union's and to international communism's genocidal nature, inherent evil and colonial policies. Let us open the eyes of all the nations to the sinister designs of Russian imperialism and the destructive lust of the Soviets. Let us open eyes of every man to the cruel plot of the human-beast against the soul and conscience of mankind.

Let us close our ranks behind the American Lithuanian Council which embraces all of us, and which marches forward on the road of liberty towards new victories.

Let us join our hands within the World Lithuanian Community which is our home away from home. Let us embrace the creativity of the Lithuanian culture, which is the nation's lifeblood and its source of vitality. Let us sustain our creative artists and help them to reflect in their creations the blessed rays of the Truth, the Beauty, and the Virtue. Let us make Lithuanian education an everyday reality.

Let us bind ourselves firmly with Lithuanian parishes so that they become not only the centers of religious, but also of national life, as well as the basis for ecclesiastic self-administration.

Let us fasten our common will into a chain of granite, which would withstand all of the communist temptations manifesting themselves under the guise of peaceful co-existence and cultural exchange. Communism is the worst enemy of every Lithuanian and indeed of every human being. All Lithuanians must fight communism by all possible and morally justifiable means. Any tendencies towards co-operation with communist exponents hide a danger to the Lithuanian nation and its fight for freedom. Let us destroy all the communist seeds of subversion which may exist among us, and which have a tendency to sow apathy in our ranks.

Let us re-dedicate ourselves to the principles of justice and order for they reflect the wisdom and love of the Almighty Creator. The Natural Order is not only the guiding principle of this earth, but of the whole universe. It is the creative ideal, reflecting the very fount of all — the Creator. All of us should strive to implement the tenets of the Natural Order, especially since exile is the issue of disorder. The Body of Law is after all the realization of Natural Order. In our civilization, Law is the basic principle of politics and statehood. It evolves out of moral precepts which in our social reality become freely created and accepted laws.

Let us show our youths the glorious heritage of Lithuanian culture. Let our relations with the younger generation be guided by open heart and mind. Let us resolve not only to speak to them but to listen as well; not only teach them, but learn from them; not only exercise leadership, but be ready to accept their counsel.

Towards the New State

Let us comprehend the mission of our nation. Let us create in our hearts and minds a Lithuanian state which would not only serve as a wedge between Eastern and Western Powers, but at the same time, provide the conditions for a birth of a new civilization which would be permeated by the best of both Eastern and Western cultures and be a beginning of a truly Christian humanism.

Let us consecrate our national concepts by the spirit of Christianity, which is not only the very energy of history, but also the force able to change the hearts of men, as well as the face of the earth.

Let us reiterate to the nation, its martyrs and fighters for freedom, its deportees and exiles, its friends and foes, the basic principles of Lithuanian statehood.

At the basis of a sovereign state is individual freedom and communal responsibility. Freedom and liberty are the most important rights of the individual, and communal responsibility is the realization of freedom dedicated to every citizen's well-being. Only when these two principles are in harmonious relationship, both the nation and the state can best serve the man whose worthiness supersedes both.

This harmonious relationship is best served by the small self-sustaining society system. It is based on the subsidiary principle in political, civic, cultural, as well as socio-economic fields, and predicated on gradualization of powers, privileges, and responsibilities in terms of power structures of different levels of state and communal organization. It means that a higher, more powerful or extensive political subdivision should not hold jurisdiction over matters or activities, which can be adequately performed by smaller political subdivision or societal entity. Such political order prevents state hegemony over its citizens, as well as facilitates the best utilization of individual and communal creativity with least amount of controls and best opportunity to serve the interests of individuals as well as those of the nation and the state, and other societal bodies.

Political democracy based upon this principle facilitates also the functioning of the entire economic structure in which the worker and his family is of prime concern. Every worker is a human being and not an economic function, and the whole socio-economic structure must be geared to serve him and his family. The worker must have the opportunity to earn a just and equitable wage commensurate with human dignity and existential needs.

The right to private property is a natural right circumscribed only by the imperatives of the public good. Every meaningful economic activity serving the consumer, the market place, and the public good, and ethically acceptable should be elevated and treated as worthy of support.

Social justice, based on the worthiness of man and the brotherhood of mankind, calls especially for a just order in the affairs of the agricultural workers. Agrarian activities must again be based on private initiative and self-administration in lieu of today's overbearing collectivism. The remuneration and working conditions of farm laborers must equal the wages and working conditions of other segments of the working force. The agricultural economy and the farm workers' interests are best served by the principle of private property ownership and meaningful organization of cooperative enterprises.

Neighborly love and brotherhood precepts originating in the depths of Christianity, mandate the principle of cultural autonomy and ideological plurality. Individual liberty and communal responsibility must be the primary guidelines in determining the cultural and ideological policies as well as the normative framework safeguarding individual expression. The most prudent, beneficial and fair way to treat those problems, which are outside the framework of politics and public administration, is to base them on the pluralistic society principle, which not only reflects the Natural Law but, also the requisites of public welfare.

201

The same principles of pluralistic society should govern the field of education since educational policies must reflect the inalienable rights and privileges of the parents.

The family is the basic unit of societal existence, national well-being, and state viability. Therefore, the family must be exposed to all potentialities, responsibilities, and privileges of the subsidiary principle. In those endeavors where the family needs special aid, the state must render such aid in the most expeditious way and in a satisfactory quantity. There are but few priorities in the sphere of public domain that supersede the legitimate needs of the family, particularly those families, whose economic means and social standing have not yet reached an adequate level.

The right to national independence is based on Natural Law. This right is also guaranteed by numerous solemn declarations as well as international covenants. National sovereignty is limited only by the inalienable human rights and by the imperatives of the well-being of the international community. Relationship between sovereign states should also be based upon the principles of freedom and international responsibility. The particular body politic decides the questions which are correlated with its sovereign rights in terms of international relationship. However, the just and meaningful federalist system is worth pursuing, since it can provide better conditions for an improved political organization, an increased economic productivity, and a wider cultural activity and creativity.

Towards Victory

We march to the battlefield with determination and courage. Our weapons are law and justice, and our goal is victory. This goal we shall never abandon. The sacrifices of our volunteer warriors of the Independence Wars, and our partisans during the struggle against communist oppression, manifest the immortality of the Lithuanian Nation. Their blood flows in our veins and will do so through coming centuries.

We march towards the future armed with a deep faith and a glorious vision. Our way is the way of creative endeavor. Our goal and our historic mission is a free and independent Lithuania.

To Christianity, Lithuanianism, Democracy!

To Lithuania!

   (s) MYKOLAS KRUPAVIČIUS
       Honorary Chairman of the
       Lithuanian Christian Democrats

   (s) ALGIRDAS J. KASULAITIS
       Chairman of the
       Lithuanian Christian Democratic Union

   (s) DR. P. KARVELIS
       Former Chairman of the
       Lithuanian Christian Democratic Party

   (s) P. VAINAUSKAS
       Former Chairman of the
       Lithuanian Christian Democratic Union

   (s) DR. K. ŠIDLAUSKAS
       Former Chairman of the
       Lithuanian Christian Democratic Union

Adopted at Cleveland, Ohio, this sixteenth day of February, in the year of our Lord, Nineteen Hundred and Sixty-Eight.[1]

ACTION PROGRAM
OF THE
LITHUANIAN CHRISTIAN DEMOCRATIC UNION
(In Exile)

I. IDEOLOGICAL FOUNDATIONS OF LITHUANIAN CHRISTIAN DEMOCRATIC UNION

1. Lithuanian Christian Democratic Union is an organization of Lithuanians who believe that the public order of Christian nations must be based on Christian principles, and who are striving to achieve such a public order.

2. The action of the Lithuanian Christian Democratic Union (in exile) is based on Christian beliefs, as well as on the belief in resurrection of Lithuania; on inherent worthiness of the Lithuanian nation; on humanism and hope of re-establishment of Lithuanian State based on the noble principles of Christianity, Lithuanianism, and Democracy.

3. As a Catholic people, Lithuanians base their public order on the social doctrines of the Catholic Church. Because Christian tenets cannot be contained only in the religious life, but must permeate all levels of man's private and public life, Christian Democracy refutes all endeavors as a manifestation of anti-Christian liberalism, which is striving, under the aegis of modernism, to eliminate Christian influence from public life.

204

4. The future of Lithuanian public order is based upon the basic needs of the nation: social justice, the experience of Christian Democracies in our countries, and realistic imperatives of present conditions.

5. In the social action field, Christian Democracy adheres to the traditionally progressive social justice rather than to the reactionary interpretation of such action.

6. Christian Democracy believes that the main basis of the socio-economic program is man and his well-being. Therefore, Christian Democracy refutes radical collectivism since it is injurious to human dignity and subscribes to the principle that in the national economic structure, capital and wealth must be subordinated to the well-being of all citizens.

II. POLITICAL AND CULTURAL PROGRAM OF LITHUANIAN CHRISTIAN DEMOCRATIC UNION

7. Political action in exile constitutes an important and inseparable part of the overall Lithuanian civic and cultural life. It is needed to sustain the Lithuanian freedom struggle; to represent political maturity; to foster Lithuanian political and national self-consciousness; and, to maintain relations with political strata of the several countries of residence. Political activity is just as necessary to nurture Lithuanian self-consciousness as the cultural one in its general manifestations. Lessening of Lithuanian political activity will have a tendency to lessen the overall activity of the several general areas of human endeavor.

8. Lithuanian Christian Democracy holds that the cultural concept embraces all progress and all fields of human endeavor, including political activity.

9. Lithuanian Christian Democrats believe that national needs supersede partisan interests and, therefore, cooperate with all groups of every political persuasion in the field of national liberation activities.

III. LITHUANIAN CHRISTIAN DEMOCRATIC UNION TASKS IN EXILE

A. *Liberation of Lithuania*

10. Until Lithuania is liberated, Lithuanian Christian Democrats hold that the fight for freedom is their main task and responsibility.

11. Participating in the political activity in connection with the freedom fight, Lithuanian Christian Democrats participate in the national political organizations and institutions and strive for unity of all patriotic political groups and their alliances.

12. Lithuanian Christian Democrats hold Soviet Communism to be the greatest enemy of freedom. Therefore, it is their duty to inform the free world of all the suffering which Communist imperialism has inflicted upon Lithuania; to call to the attention of the free world the dangers of Communist imperialism in general; to aid anti-communist forces; to join in the free world's struggle against Communism by actively participating in anti-communist demonstrations, exhibits, discussions, etc.

13. Christian Democrats actively oppose defeatist tendencies in the society as well as Communist attempts to extinguish anti-communist resolve and the struggle for independence.

B. *Preparation for Lithuania's Re-Establishment*

14. Christian Democrats must prepare themselves for the re-establishement of free Lithuania. For that purpose, they study the present conditions in captive Lithuania, its social and other changes, and based on realistic analysis, plan the future of the Lithuanian State.

15. Lithuanian Christian Democratic Union considers its duty to foster Christian Democracy and to prepare for its resurgence in free and independent Lithuania.

C. *Fostering Lithuanianism*

16. Based upon Lithuanian vision of the future, Lithuanian Christian Democratic Union considers it its responsibility to strive for education of Lithuanian youth in terms of Lithuanian self-consciousness. It is the aim of Lithuanian Christian Democratic Union that the younger generation be patriotic and motivated to join in the activities of re-establishment of free Lithuania.

17. Every Christian Democrat considers it his duty to participate in Lithuanian affairs, to aid Lithuanian educational institutions, and to join in unified efforts seeking the above mentioned aims.

D. *Dissemination of Christian Democratic Information*

18. Christian Democrats must organize Lithuanian Christian Democratic chapters wherever possible, and be actively engaged in their work, representing Christian Democracy, and disseminating Christian Democratic information throughout the community.

19. For the purpose of continuing the liberation struggle, and for the benefit of the general Lithuanian acti-

vities, as well as for the nurturing of the Christian Democratic ideals, it is necessary that the youth be inducted into the activities of Lithuanian Christian Democratic Union.

IV. THE IMPERATIVES OF LITHUANIAN CHRISTIAN DEMOCRATIC UNION ACTION

20. Christian Democracy, which has such noble and firm set of principles, necessitates also a corresponding responsibility and action on the part of leaders and membership, for the promulgation of its ideas. Any shortcomings in practical life are not caused by the Christian Democratic precepts, but by the inactivity of the leadership or of individual members of the Union.

21. The exile population has a tendency to lose political enthusiasm. For this reason, Christian Democracy and its proponents must possess aggressive creativeness, dedication, and high moral standards.

22. Present conditions and the dispersion of Lithuanians throughout the world prevent Christian Democrats from performing certain functions effectively. This situation poses special tasks for the leadership as well as for every member of the Lithuanian Christian Democratic Union. Therefore, it is the duty of every Christian Democrat to work for Lithuanian and Christian Democratic causes according to a particular set of circumstances prevalent at a specific time and place.

23. Christian Democracy as a political movement, cannot limit either its interests or concern to any class or profession, but must embrace all people without prejudice to education, race, class, or social strata, etc.

208

(Paragraphs 24, 25, and 26 which describe in detail organizational matters are left out because of their technical nature. This Lithuanian Christian Democratic Union Program which is in effect at this time, was adopted by the Central Committee of the Lithuanian Christian Democratic Union on June 2, 1962).²

MEMORANDUM

LITHUANIA UNDER THE SOVIET
TIONAL PARTIES, AND YOUTH MOVE-
TO ALL CHRISTIAN DEMOCRATIC IN-
TERNATIONAL ORGANIZATIONS, NA-
MENTS

ON

THE PLIGHT OF THE REPUBLIC OF
UNION OCCUPATION

Gentlemen:

June 15th marks another tragic anniversary of the occupation of Lithuania by Soviet Russia 26 years ago. It is tragic because even until this time Lithuania, as well as other Baltic countries, are still under the yoke of international Communism directed by the Kremlin.

The Lithuanian Christian Democratic Union in exile, as well as all Lithuanians in the free world, continue to wage a relentless fight for the freedom of their country and for the liberty of its people. We hope that in this fight we are not alone.

We note, with deep concern, that all superficial changes notwithstanding, Lithuania's plight under the occupation has not changed. Indeed, in some ways it has worsened considerably.

Politically, Lithuania is still under the severest control of the Central Government of the Soviet Union. All political parties are outlawed and their leaders either exterminated or still held in prisons. The country is ruled by Moscow through its emissaries and through its few Lithuanian puppet functionaries. This governing apparatus is backed up by the Soviet Army and by Russian police garrisons stationed on Lithuanian soil.

Economic exploitation continues unabated. In reality, Lithuania serves the Soviet Union as a manufacturer and supplier of goods. Shortages of the most common consumer goods in Lithuania is still acute. Even in those areas of economy in which Lithuania used to excel and export, the country is now experiencing irreparable shortages.

The industrial and agricultural workers are held in severe economic bondage. Wages and salaries are of subsistence level without any consideration for human dignity and the right of workers to provide for their families. All democratic labor unions are outlawed. The right to choose work does not exist. All facets of labor-management relations are controlled by the government for the government.

Cultural tyranny is evident in all the arts and sciences. Literature, art, music, and indeed the Lithuanian language and its folklore are rigidly controlled by the Communist usurpers. The written word, the canvas, and the symphony are subjugated to the political and imperialistic task to fulfill the cultural genocidal purposes of Soviet Russia.

Genocide is still practiced by most refined methods. Russification manifests itself in schools, offices, organizations, publications, news media, and all other facets of life.

Schools are subservient to the Communist doctrine and the devious purposes of the occupying power. The sacred right of parents in the field of education is null and void in Lithuania today. The children are still forced to spy on their parents and report their activities to the authorities.

211

Religious persecution is of late increased and intensified. More than half of the Lithuanian clergy are exterminated. Majority of churches are closed. During the past quarter of a century, not a single publication of any consequence was published.

Many thousands of Lithuanians are still held in slave labor camps and prisons in Siberia and other places. They are only a fraction of the million Lithuanian nationals murdered during the past 26 years in methodical genocide of the populous.

These few paragraphs cannot describe the injustice, degradation, and exploitation of Lithuania. Such behavior by the Soviet Union is against every and all principles of the Charter of the United Nations and its Universal Declaration on Human Rights. Indeed, it is against the Law of God and the conscience of the Free World.

We ask your help in this fight for freedom and liberty. Do not do anything in your party's activities which would dim the lights of hope for occupied Lithuania. Petition your governments to work for peace with justice for all. Raise your mighty voices in international gatherings for the cause of freedom for all enslaved nations. Use your good offices everywhere in the cause for human dignity.

We strongly believe that no nation can be free until all nations are free. All we ask is freedom for our nation; the right to guide our own destiny; the right to participate in the community of nations for the betterment of mankind; and, the right to build a brighter future based on everlasting principles of Christian Democracy.

(s) ALGIRDAS J. KASULAITIS,
President
Central Committee

June 15, 1967

AN APPEAL TO THE AMERICAN PEOPLE
CONCERNING FREEDOM FOR
SOVIET OCCUPIED LITHUANIA

This year marks the fiftieth anniversary of the restoration of the independence of Lithuania, once an ancient civilization, whose roots go back to the second century, and a modern Republic, whose political, economic and social record was as distinctive as it was progressive. It is tragic therefore, that this anniversary is overshadowed by the brutal fact that Lithuania today is under the yoke of the Soviet Union.

The tragedy commenced with the Soviet-Nazi conspiracy at the outbreak of World War II, when the two imperialist powers in the most despicable way sowed destruction and death upon entire nations and millions of people. The infamous Molotov-Ribbentrop Pacts, together with the Secret Protocols, amply document how Lithuania and other peace-loving nations were victimized by brute force and international immorality. (See "Nazi-Soviet Relations 1939-1941", excerpts attached).

There was not even a shadow of legality to the occupation. The gun and the tank replaced law and international obligations. No less than four bilateral treaties were broken by the Kremlin, when its Red hordes marched upon Lithuania:

> The Treaty of Brest-Litovsk of March 3, 1919 in which the Soviet Union forever renounced all claims to Lithuania;

213

The Peace Treaty of July 12, 1920 which defined the common boundaries;

The Non-Aggression Pact of September 28, 1928 which was later extended to 1945, and

The Mutual Assistance Pact of October 10, 1939.

Occupation was followed by systematic terror and violence, which in many forms continues to this day, all superficial changes notwithstanding.

Politically Lithuania is still under the severest control of the central government of the Soviet Union, which is backed up by the Red Army and Russian police garrisons stationed on Lithuanian soil. Economic exploitation continues unabated. The industrial and agricultural workers are held in severe economic bondage. Cultural tyrrany is evident in all the arts and sciences. Genocide is still practiced by the most refined methods. Schools are subservient to the Communist doctrine and the devious purposes of the occupying power. Religous persecution has of late increased and intensified. Many thousands of Lithuanians are still imprisoned for crimes they never committed.

These few paragraphs cannot describe the injustice, degradation and exploitation of Lithuania. Such behaviour by the Soviet Union is against every and all principles of the United Nations and its Universal Declaration of Human Rights. Indeed it is against the Law of God and the conscience of the World Community.

On July 23, 1940 the United States denounced this naked aggression against Lithuania and other Baltic countries. All Administrations since then affirmed this stand and spoke unequivocally against this brutal invasion.

It is difficult to conceive that during the present rise of many former colonial countries to their rightly deserved national independences, a shroud of silence is maintained about Lithuania and the other countries whose traditions of statehood reach back for centuries.

It is even more difficult to conceive that all the international crimes perpetrated by the Soviet Union are still not rectified, nor the perpetrator punished. It is indeed a crime in itself that Kremlin is still permitted to indulge in international rape, the latest victim being Czechoslovakia, just a few short weeks ago.

In this election year, when the American people will exercise one of the basic freedoms that are denied to all Kremlin enslaved nations, let us not forget that no nation is truly free until all nations are free. Hollow words are no substitute for action.

We suggest crusade for international morality and decency, for international law and order, for responsibility and action, for true brotherhood and true peace.

We appeal to all Americans for help in our fight for liberty and justice. We appeal especially to those officeholders and candidates in whose hands rests the fate not only of this country, but to a large measure the future of the world. We appeal in behalf of those millions of enslaved people who are voiceless, to the millions who are the hope of tommorow.

(s) A. J. KASULAITIS, President
Central Committee

(s) K. ALGIMANTAS PAUTIENIS, Chairman
Commission on International Relations

October, 1968.

RESOLUTION CONCERNING THE SITUATION
OF ALL NATIONS ENSLAVED BY SOVIET RUSSIA

(Adopted by the Third World Congress of UIJDC, Montevideo)

1. Every nation, as well as, every man has a God-given natural right to national freedom and individual liberty. This most precious right has been time and again reaffirmed by the great Charters of International Law, the United Nations, and the Declaration of Human Rights.

2. This sacred right has been and still is most flagrantly violated in the enslaved countries of Eastern and Middle Europe.

3. The Baltic States which were occupied a quarter of a century ago by the brute military force of the imperialist Soviet Union, are still being held in most severe bondage. All religious, political, cultural and other rights do not exist. A great number of citizens of these countries have been exterminated in prisons and slave labor camps. Economic exploitation has reached the level of serfdom. The common life is completely void of any human dignity and right.

4. The Congress deplores and condemns any, every and all violations against freedom and liberty wherever it exists. It solemnly reaffirms its dedication to the inalienable human rights and national self-determination.

5. The Congress appeals to all nations and all governments to take any and all necessary measures in behalf of the enslaved nations.

6. The Congress pledges its common effort in unstinting toil for freedom and liberty for all. In this solemn declaration the Congress again reaffirms its belief in the redeeming and everlasting principles of universal Christian Democracy dedicated to the sacred brotherhood of man under the Fatherhood of Almighty God.

LITHUANIAN
CHRONOLOGY

XIII CENTURY

Period of amalgamation of the several Lithuanian
    principalities under Mindaugas   1219-1236
Establishment of Lithuanian Kingdom   1251
War with the Tartars   1258
Defeat of the Order of the Sword   1260
Teutonic Order conquers Prussia   1282

XIV CENTURY

Grand Duke Gediminas establishes Vilnius as
    capital of Lithuania   1323
Grand Duke Algirdas defeats the Tartars and
    establishes his rule over Ukraine   1362
Jogaila becomes the King of Poland   1386
Lithuania is baptized   1387

XV CENTURY

Vytautas the Great (Lithuanians and Poles) defeats
    the Teutonic Order   1410
Principality of Moscow reorganized by Lithuania   1449
Wars with Moscow   1499-1582

XVI CENTURY

First book printed in Lithuanian   1534
Livonia united with Lithuania   1561

Lithuanian-Polish Commonwealth established
    at the meeting of Lublin   1569
Vilnius Academy founded   1579
Lithuanian law codified into the Lithuanian Statute,
    published in three successive editions   1529-66-68

XVII CENTURY

Sweden defeated by Lithuania   1605
Lithuanian-Polish condominium of Livonia
    ceded to Sweden   1629

XVIII CENTURY

Wars with Sweden   1701-1709
Famine and pestilence in Lithuania   1708-1711
First partition of Lithuania and Poland   1772
Reform of education in Lithuania   1773
Second partition of Lithuania and Poland   1793
Insurrection against Russian rule led by Lithuanian
    General T. Kosciuszko   1794
Third partition of Lithuania and Poland   1795

XIX CENTURY

Lithuania joins Napoleon in the war against Russia 1812
Insurrection against Russia   1831
Russians close the University of Vilnius   1832
Serfdom abolished   1861
Insurrection against Russia   1863
Lithuanian printing in Latin characters outlawed 1864

First Lithuanian newspaper *"Aušra"* published
in East Prussia   1883
Lithuanian Christian Democratic Movement
organized   1887
The Great Lithuanian massacre at Kražiai
by the Russians   1893

XX CENTURY

The ban on Lithuanian printing lifted   1904
Lithuanian revolt against the Russians   1905
The Grand Congress of Vilnius   1905
The Conference of Vilnius   1917
Declaration of Independence (February 16th)   1918
Wars of Independence against Poland, Germany,
and Russia   1918-1920
Elections to the Constituent Assembly   1920
Peace Treaty with the Soviet Union   1920
Non-Aggression Pact with the Soviet Union   1926
Secret Soviet-Nazi agreements against Lithuania 1939
Soviet invasion and occupation of Lithuania (June 15) 1940
First mass deportations   (June 15-16) 1941
Lithuania revolts against Soviet Russia   (June 22) 1941
Lithuania under German occupation   1941-1944
Supreme Committee for Liberation of Lithuania
is organized   1943
Second Soviet occupation of Lithuania   1944
Lithuanian guerilla warfare against Russia   1944-1952

NOTES

1. PHYSIOGRAPHY

1. Cf. Dr. V. Vladas (pseudonym of Dr. Vladas Viliamas), "Country and Population" in Lithuania, edited by Dr. A. Stanys (pseudonym of Dr. Adolfas Šapoka), (Augsburg, 1946), pp. 3-4. For in-depth study of the subject cf. V. Čepulytė, Lietuvos žemės paviršius, (Vilnius, 1957), and A. Basalykas, ed. Lietuvos fizinė geografija, I and II volumes (Vilnius, 1958-65). Also K. Pakštas, Baltijos Respublikų politinė geografija (Kaunas, 1929).
88,000 square kilometers — km.² (1 km.² equals 0.386 square mile.

3. The subject of Lithuania's area (political and ethnographic) is a complicated matter. Although linguistic, historic, ethnographic, cultural, archeological and related studies quite clearly establish Lithuanian ethnographic boundaries ,political circumstances before and after Lithuanian declaration of independence prevented Lithuania from exercising sovereignty over the area belonging to her. Even international treaties signed by Lithuania and her neighbors up to 1924 theoretically normalizing the Republic's boundaries, were broken as soon as they were signed (by Poland and later Germany and the USSR). For authoritative studies on the subject cf. Dr. K. Pakštas work cited above and "Changing Population in Lithuania", Lituanus, 1957, No. 1; "Keletas samprotavimų apie Lietuvos ribas", Aidai, 1950, Nos. 1 through 4; "Lietuvių Tautos plotai ir gyventojai", Aidai, 1957, No. 3; "National and State Boundaries", Lituanus, 1959, No. 3, p. 67.

4. Cf. Dr. V. Vladas, op. cit., p. 3.

5. Ibid., p. 5. For in-depth study cf. K. Pakštas, Le Climat de la Lituanie (Klaipėda, 1926).

6. Ibid.

7. See Note 3.

2. POPULATION

1. Includes the Vilnius region. Cf. Dr. V. Vladas, op. cit., p. 6.

2. Cf. V. Vaitiekūnas, Lithuania (New York, 1968), p. 7. P Zundė in Lituanus (No. 3-4, 1964) pegs the population loss at 1,090,000 people. Dr. Pakštas estimates the losses at "over a million" people, (Lithuania and World War II, Chicago, 1947,

222

p. 43. Other studies also put the figure between one million and 1.3 million people.

3. Dr. V. Vladas, op. cit., p. 6.

4. For Russianization of the Lithuanian vocabulary under the Soviets cf. Antanas Salys' article in Lituanus, 1967, No. 2, pp. 47-62. This issue has also several other articles on Lithuanian language including "A bibliography of Works Dealing with the Relationship between Baltic and Slavic" by Gary A. Hood.

5. Cf. P. Jonikas, Lietuvių kalbos istorija (History of the Lithuanian Language), Chicago, 1952.

6. Antanas Klimas, "The Importance of Lithuanian for Indo-European Linguistics", Lituanus, 1969, No. 3, p. 10. The same issue of the magazine has several other scholarly articles on Lithuanian language by Professor Klimas (University of Rochester), as well as, Professor William R. Schmalstieg (The Pennsylvania State University).

7. Cf. E. J. Harrison, Lithuania's Fight for Freedom), New York, 1952, pp. 6-7.

8. Ibid.

3. HISTORICAL OUTLINE

1. The author is indebted to his history teacher, the late and eminent historian Dr. Adolfas Šapoka, whose synopsis of Lithuanian history is followed in this outline. Cf. Lithuania (Augsburg, 1946).

2. Cf. Lietuvių Enciklopedija (hereafter referred to as LE), Vol. XVIII, pp. 493-502.

3. Cf. Dr. Viktoras Gidžiūnas, O.F.M., "The Introduction of Christianity in Lithuania", Lituanus, 1957, No. 4(13), p. 7.

4. Cf. Dr. Joseph B. Koncius, Vytautas the Great, Grand Duke of Lithuania (Miami, Fla., 1964). Also LE, Vol. XXXIV, pp. 373-537.

5. Cf. Encyclopedia Lituanica (hereafter referred to as EL), Vol. II, pp. 533-537.

6. Cf. Juozas Jakštas, "Glugosz About the Battle of Tannenberg", Lituanus, 1962, No. 3, p. 71. — — —, "The Battle of Tannenberg, 1410", The Baltic Review, No. 20, p. 19; and Constantine R. Jurgėla, Ph. D., Tannenberg (New York, 1961).

7. For general textbooks on Lithuanian history cf. A. Šapoka, ed., Lietuvos Istorija, 3rd edition (Fellbach-Wuerttenberg, 1950); V. Daugirdaitė-Sruogienė, Lietuvos Istorija, 6th edition, (Chicago), both in Lithuanian; and Constantine Jurgela, History of Lithuania (New York, 1948), in English.

4. POLITICAL, SOCIAL AND ECONOMIC CONDITIONS IN THE XIX CENTURY

1. Dr. Vanda Sruoga, "Lithuanian Statute", **Lituanus**, 1959 No. 4, p. 121.
2. Cf. EL, Vol. II, pp. 469-471; LE, Vol. XII, pp. 475-478.
3. Cf. Pranas Čepėnas, "The Lithuanian Revolt of 1831", **Lituanus**, 1956, No. 3, p. 16; EL, Vol. II, pp. 471-474; LE, Vol. XXIX, pp. 133-147.
4. Cf. V. Trumpa, "The 1863 Revolt in Lithuania", **Lituanus**, 1963, No. 4, p. 115; EL, Vol. II, pp. 474-478; LE, Vol. XXIX, pp. 148-165. For a critical review of present day Communist interpretation of the 1863 revolt, cf. J. Jakštas, "The 1863 Revolt in Soviet Historiography", **Lituanus**, 1963, No. 4, p. 145. The eminent Lithuanian historian briefly but incisively refutes the ideas propounded in several recent Lithuanian Communist works on the 1863 revolt.
5. Cf. A. Šapoka, **Lietuvos Istorija**, p. 457.

5. THE FIRST SEEDS OF CHRISTIAN DEMOCRACY

1. Cf. LE, Vol. XXIX, pp. 28-32.
2. Cf. EL, Vol. I, pp. 290-293; LE, Vol. II, pp. 185-191.
3. Cf. LE, Vol. XXXIII, pp. 536-538.
4. Certain periods in the evolvement of Lithuanian Christian Democratic thought was first suggested by Msgr. Mykolas Krupavičius in an interview. Cf. **Tėvynės Sargas** (hereafter referred to as **TS**), 1954, No. 1(11), p. 6 et seq.
5. Ibid. p. 8.
6. Ibid. Cf. also LE, Vol. XXXII, pp. 523-531.
7. Interchangeably called Diocese of Medininkai or Samogitia (Lith. Žemaičiai). For an authoritative study on the diocese see Zenonas Ivinskis, "Žemaičių (Medininkų) vyskupijos įkūrimas (1417) ir jos reikšmė lietuvių tautai, (1417-1967)", (Medininkai — The Bishopric of Samogitia (Žemaičiai), its Founding (1417) and Significance for Lithuania (1417-1967)", **The Proceedings of the 7th Congress of the Lithuanian Catholic Science Academy**, Rome, 1972, pp. 55-130. (In Lithuanian).
8. See Note 4, Chapter 4.
9. Cf. EL, Vol. III, pp. 443-445.
10. See Note 4, Chapter 4.

6. THE BEGINNING OF THE MOVEMENT

1. Cf. J. J. Stukas, **Awakening Lithuania** (Madison, N. J., 1966). Kun. Vyt. Bagdanavičius, MIC, Editor, **Kovos metai dėl savrᵢ sios spaudos** (Chicago, 1957).
2. Cf. LE, Vol. III, pp. 147-150; EL, Vol. I, pp. 384-385.
3. Cf. EL, Vol. I, pp. 216-218; LE, Vol. I, pp. 465-473; Kun. Vyt. Bagdanavičius, op. cit.
4. Cf. EL, Vol. I, pp. 307-310; LE, Vol. II, pp. 241-247.
5. Msgr. Mykolas Krupavičius, op. cit., p. 9.
6. Ibid.
7. Cf. LE, Vol. XXI, pp. 366-367.
8. Petras-Pranciškus Būčys (Bishop), "Prieš senajam 'Tėvynės Sargui' užgemant", (Jaunų dienų prisiminimai), (Before the Old TS was born-Recollections of the Younger Days), **TS**, 1947, No. 1, pp. 2-7; St. Dzikas, "Tėvynės Sargybon prieš 60 metų", (To the Guardpost of Homeland 60 Years Ago), **TS**, 1956, No. 1(13), pp. 1-6; Rev. F. Lialis, "Pirmojo 'Tėvynės Sargo' redaktoriaus atsiminimai", (Recollections of the First Editor of TS). Reprinted from "**Mūsų Senovė**", Books 4-5, 1922, **TS**, 1966. No. 1(27), pp. 21-34.
9. Cf. LE, Vol. XXXII, pp. 27-34.
10. Cf. **Christian Democracy in Central Europe** (New York, 1952), p. 44.
11. Antanas Vaičiulaitis, ~~Outline~~ History of Lithuanian Literature (Chicago, 1942), p. 30.
12. Cf. LE, Vol. XXXIII, pp. 167-174.

7. ADOPTATION OF THE FIRST FORMAL PROGRAM

1. For the more detailed, in some cases eyewitness reports on this period of Lithuanian Christian Democracy's growth (just before the Grand Congress in Vilnius in 1905) cf. Prel. Kaz. Šau- of the Past, Activities of Lithuanian Christian Democrats by Rev. J. Tumas), **TS**, 1949, No. 2-3(6-7), p. 118, reprint from "**Draugija**", (The Society), 1907, No. 3, pp. 257-266. lys, "Iš atsiminimų apie krikščioniškąją demokratiją Lietuvoje" (Some Recollections About Christian Democracy in Lithuania, by Msgr. Kaz. Šaulys), **TS**, 1948, No 4, p. 258; Kun. J. Tumas, "Iš praeities, lietuvių krikščionių demokratų veikimas" (Out
2. For a complete text in Lithuanian (with but a few inconsequential deletions) see **TS**, 1949, No. 2-3 (6-7), pp. 125-132.

Substantial experts were taken from this text and translated by the author.

3. For interrelationship between the Lithuanian National Reawakening and democratic ideas cf. K. Čeginskas' study in V. Bagdanavičius, ed. **Kovos metai dėl savosios spaudos** (Lithuania's Fight for a Free Press), (Chicago, 1957), p. 105 et seq.

4. Cf. **EL**, Vol. III, pp. 450-453.

5. Cf. **EL**, Vol. II, pp. 16-17.

6. Cf. **Vyskupo P. P. Bučio Atsiminimai** (Bishop P. P. Bučys Memoirs), Vols. I and II, (Chicago, 1966); (Msgr.) F(eliksas) B(artk)us, "Jo Excelencija Vyskupas Petras Pranciškus Bučys", **TS**, 1949, No. 2-3 (6-7), pp. 86-94.

7. For historical notes on the program see also: M. Krupavičius, "Krikščioniškoji Demokratija Lietuvoje" (Christian Democracy in Lithuania), TS, 1954, No. 1(11), p. 10 et seq.; Prel. K. Šaulys, "Lietuvių Krikščionių Demokratų Susivienijimo Programos projektas" (A Draft of the Program of the Lithuanian Christian Democratic Alliance), **TS**, 1954, No. 1(11), pp. 65-66. Although the Program was drafted in 1904, and it was used by Christian Democrats in the Great Congress of Vilnius in 1905, it first appeared in print of general distribution only in the January 1, 1907 issue of "**Draugija**" (The Society): see **TS**, qtd. above, p. 10.

8. THE BIRTH OF THE PARTY

1. Cf. Jonas Dainauskas, "Prelude to Independence: The Great Conference of Vilnius, 1905", **Lituanus**, 1965, No. 4, p. 47 et seq.; Petras-Pranciškus Bučys, MIC, "Šį tą prisimenant iš Didžiojo Vilniaus seimo" (Remembering Something from the Great Congress of Vilnius), **TS**, 1948, No. 4, p. 254 et seq.

2. Jonas Dainauskas, op. cit., p. 53.

3. P. P. Bučys, op. cit., p. 255; Jonas Dainauskas, op. cit., p. 55.

4. For the full text of the Resolutions adopted by the Congress see Jonas Dainauskas, op. cit., p. 56 et seq.

5. Jonas Dainauskas, op. cit., p. 58.

6. Ibid., p. 60

7. Cf. P. P. Bučys, op. cit.

8. Cf. S. Senkonis, "Lietuvos kairiųjų partijų užuomazga ir pasaulėžiūriniai jų pagrindai" (The beginnings and ideological bases of Lithuania's leftist Parties), **TS**, 1952, No. 2(9), pp.224-242.

(Thes Second State Conference and its Goals), TS, 1949, No.
9. Cf. Prel. K. Šaulys, "Iš atsiminimų...", p. 259.
10. Cf. M. Krupavičius, "Krikščioniškoji Demokratija...", p. 23;
Kun. J. Tumas, "Iš praeities...", p. 120 et seq.
11. Cf. Kun. J. Tumas, "Iš praeities...", p. 124.
12. Father (later Msgr.) Aleksandras Dambrauskas-Jakštas.
13. See Note 7, Chapter 8.

9. TOWARDS INDEPENDENCE

1. M. Krupavičius, "Krikščioniškoji demokratija...", p. 35.
2. Cf. Bernardas Žukauskas, **Pirmojo pasaulinio karo tremty, (In**
Exile During First World War), (Chicago, 1960), p. 84.
3. Ibid., p. 64 et seq.
4. Ibid., p. 79.
5. M. Krupavičius, "Krikščioniškoji Demokratija...", p. 37.
6. Ibid.
7. Ibid., p. 39.
8. Ibid.
9. Cf. M. Krupavičius, "Aleksandras Stulginskis mano atsimini-
muose", (Aleksandras Stulginskis in my Recollections), TS,
1948, No. 1, p. 66.
10. Cf. L. Patvara, "Antroji valstybės konferencija ir jos uždaviniai",
2-3 (6-7), p. 161 et seq.
11. Ibid.
12. Ibid.
13. 14 representatives out of the total of 112, Cf. P. V. Raulinaitis,
"Lietuvos Darbo Federacijos įsikūrimas ir veikla Lietuvos Seimų laikais", (The Inception of the Labor Federation of Lithuania and its Activities During the Parliamentary Period), TS,
1955, No. 2, p. 64, et. seq.
14. One of the main reasons for the Federation's existence was
the Socialdemocratic Party's activities among the laboring class.
To counterbalance the Socialist and Marxist influence a Party
was needed that workers could relate to without having to
compromise or give-up their Christian principles. Hence the
Federation and its success.

10. THE CONSTITUENT ASSEMBLY

1. Cf. Dr. V. Viliamas, "Lietuvos seimai ir jų grupinė dife-
rencijacija" (Lithuanian Diets and their political differentiation), TS, 1954, No. 1(11), p. 78.

2. Ibid., p. 79.
3. Ibid., p. 80.
4. Ibid.
5. Ibid.
6. Ibid., pp. 84-85.
7. Ibid., p. 88.
8. Ibid., p. 89. The above cited Dr. Viliamas' study (71 page in four TS issues) is one of the most authoritative analysis of the Constituent Assembly, as well as, the three following Diets, with an accent on Christian Democratic activities. The most extensive source on the subject are **Lietuvos Seimų stenogramos** (Stenographic Record of the Lithuanian Diets), a 12 volume record of the work of the Diets. It can be found in the New York Public Library. Valuable material can also be found in a special issue of **TS** (1970, No. 1-31) commemorating the 50th anniversary of the Constituent Assembly. Over 130 pages of the magazine are devoted to several articles and essays by Dr. Viliamas, Lithuania's Charge d'Affairs in Washington The Hon. J. Kajeckas, Chairman of the Supreme Committee for Liberation of Lithuania Dr. J. K. Valiūnas, Bishop V. Brizgys, former Prime Minister of the Provisional Government of 1941 Col. K. Škirpa, longtime diplomat and later longtime President of Committee for a Free Lithuania V. Sidzikauskas, former Minister of the Provisional Government of 1941 Mečys Mackevičius, member of the 3rd Diet and longtime President of Lithuanian American Council Leonardas Šimutis, J.B. Laučka, prof. Konstantinas Račkauskas and others.

II. THE CONSTITUTION

1. Dr. V. Viliamas, op. cit., p. 97.
2 Ibid., p. 99.
3. For the full text of the Constitution cf. Konstantinas Račkauskas, **Lietuvos konstitucinės teisės klausimais** (On the Questions of Lithuania's Constitutional Law), New York, 1967. In this book the late Dr. Račkauskas, longtime Fordham University professor of comparative constitutional law, international relations, and international law presents a scholarly analysis of Lithuanian Constitutions of 1922, 1928 and 1938, their similarities and differences and treatment of selected provisions and articles in them.

228

12. THE LAND REFORM

1. "I remember when during the period 1922 to 1926 the Christian Democrats of Lithuania through Msgr. Krupavičius accomplished the land reform raising the nation into a high plane of economic well-being, which together with the school reform in a short time empowered Lithuania to achieve a high cultural, as well as, enviable social well-being level". De Gasperi further said: "It can't be forgotten that under your leader Msgr. Krupavičius, the Christian Democratic members of the Diet created a structure of laws that together with the Constitution of the Republic governed the country's life and created one of the most democratic Constitutions in Europe." ("Jaunimo Žygiai", 1959, No. 1(18), pp. 15 and 16.)
2. Cf. **TS**, 1949, No. 2-3 (6-7), pp. 125-132.
3. Cf. M. Krupavičius, "Krikščioniškoji demokratija...", p. 47.
4. Ibid.
5. Ibid.
6. Ibid.
7. Cf. Pranas Pauliukonis, "Prelatas Mykolas Krupavičius ir žemės reforma" (Msgr. Mykolas Krupavičius and the Land Reform), **TS**, 1969, No. 1 (30), p. 105. (The essay continued through three **TS** issues: 1968, No. 1 (29), 1969, No. 1(30) and 1971, No. 1 (32).)
8. Ibid.
9. Dr. Vl. Viliamas, "Lietuvos seimai...", p. 90.
10. M. Krupavičius, op. cit., p. 92.
11. Ibid.
12. Ibid.
13. Ibid.
14. Ibid., p. 93.
15. Cf. Pr Pauliukonis, op. cit., p. 46.
16. By the Nationalist Government decree.
17. Cf. **EL**, Vol. I, p. 36.
18. Cf. Pr. Pauliukonis, op. cit., p. 46.
19. Cf. **EL**, Vol. I, p. 36.
20. Ibid.
21. .J Jatulionis and A. Mažiulis, "Economic Relations in Lithuania", **Lithuania**, ed. Dr. A. Stanys, Augsburg, 1946, p. 51.
22. M. Krupavičius, op. cit., p. 50.
23. The flavor of the period regarding the land reform is very capably captured in "Žemės reforma beldžiasi" (The Land Re-

form is Knocking), a fragment of memoirs by a well known poet, the late Canon Mykolas Vaitkus. Cf. **TS**, 1949, No. 2-3 (6-7), pp. 143-157. An abbreviated English version of Pranas Pauliukonis' (the late historian) essay on the topic can be found in **Lituanus**, 1970, No. 4, pp. 31-46, ("Mykolas Krupavičius and the Lithuanian Land Reform").

13. THE FIRST AND SECOND DIETS

1. The merger was announced in the Diet on November 24, 1922.
2. Cf. Dr. V. Viliamas, op. cit., **TS**, 1955, No. 2 (12), p. 57.
3. December 21, 1922.
4. Cf. D.V. Viliamas, op. cit.
4. Cf. D.V. Viliamas, op. cit., p. 60.
5. Ibid.
6. Ibid., p. 63.
7. Ibid.
8. Cf. Dr. V. Viliamas, op. cit., **TS**, 1956, No. 1 (13), p. 51.
9. Ibid., p. 55.
10. Ibid., p. 57.
11. Ibid., p. 59.
12. Ibid.
13. Ibid., p. 61.

14. OTHER ACHIEVEMENTS

1. Cf. Dr. V. Viliamas, op. cit., **TS**, 1954, No. 1 (11), pp. 93-97.
2. Ibid.
3. Ibid.
4. M. Krupavičius, op. cit., p. 52.
5. Ibid.
6. Cited from prof. Kazys Pakštas, Ph. D, **Lithuania and World WAR II** (Chicago 1947) p. 69 (Translation by the Secretariat of the League of Nations)
7. Article 1. Cited from Domas Krivickas analysis "Lithuania's Struggle Against Aggression and Subjugation" in **Twenty Years' Struggle for Freedom of Lithuania**, ed. Juozas Audėnas (New York, 1963), p. 125.
8. Ibid.
9. For the story of Vilnius from its origins to today, cf. Adolfas Šapoka, Ph. D., **Vilnius in the Life of Lithuania**, (Toronto, 1962).

10. For an overview of Lithuanian-Polish relations cf. Simas Su-
žiedėlis essay in **Lietuva** magazine, 1954 No. 6, pp. 81-99.
11. For a complete chronological list cf. M. Krupavičius, "Nepr.
Lietuvos Respublikos pripažinimai de facto ir de jure" (Recogni-
tions of the Independent Republic of Lithuania de facto and
de jure), **TS**, 1968, No. 1 (29), pp. 18-20.

15. MYKOLAS KRUPAVIČIUS — A BUILDER OF A NATION

1. Cf. Vyt. Bagdanavičius, M.I.C., "Krupavičiaus kunigystė", **TS**,
1972, No. 1 (32), p. 10-31.
2. Cf. Kun. K. Šaulys, "Nepakeičiamas seiminis kalbėtojas" (Ir-
replacable Parliamentary Orator), **TS**, 1955, No. 2 (12), p. 22.
3. The following are Msgr. Krupavičius' more important books and
essays:

> **Kokia mums reikalinga mokykla** (What Type of
> School do we need), Kaunas, 1919.
> **Dangaus šviesa Leonas XIII** (Leo XIII — Light
> from Heaven), Kaunas, 1920, 2nd ed. 1929.
> **Žemės reformų klausimas Lietuvos politinių partijų
> programose.** (Question of Land reforms in Lithuania's
> Political Parties' Programs), Kaunas, 1920.
> **Mūsų keliai** (Our Ways), Kaunas, 1921.
> **Rinkimai** (The Elections), Kaunas, 1925.
> **Lietuvių politinės partijos** (Lithuanian Political Par-
> ties), Kaunas, 1921.
> **Krikščioniškoji Demokratija** (Christian Democracy),
> Stuttgart, Germany, 1948.
> **Lietuviškoji Išeivija** (Lithuanian Exile), Italy, 1959.
> "Nauja pasaulio santvarka" (The New World Order),
> **Yearbook** of the Lithuanian Catholic Academy of
> Sciences, Vol. I, Rome, 1965.

(After arrest by the Nazis Msgr. Krupavičius left in Lithuania three unpublished books: **Darbas ir kapitalas** (Labor
and Capital), **Liturginis katekizmas** (Liturgical Catechism),
and **Prie Kristaus kojų** (At the Feet of Christ). After his death,
the inventory of his papers yielded some more manuscripts: a
collection of 40 essays on Christian Sociology, monography on
Kalvarija (a town in Lithuania), etc.

4. There is already some literature on the life and work of
Msgr. Krupavičius, besides his own **Memoirs** encampassing the

period from his youth to 1919. (**Atsiminimai**, Chicago, 1972).
The book was published posthumously by the executors of
his last will. The most extensive monography on his life and
work by Petras Maldeikis was published recently. Among
some more comprehensive essays cf. Dr. D. Jasaitis, "Mykolas
Krupavičius, visuomenininkas, politikas ir kovotojas" (M.K. Civic Leader, Political leader and Fighter), **TS**, 1955, No. 2 (12),
pp. 1-22, and J. Matulionis, "Mykolas Krupavičius", **TS**, 1961,
No. 1 (20) pp. 1-15.

16. A GALLERY OF STATESMEN

1. Cf. M. Krupavičius, "Aleksandras Stulginskis mano atsimini-
   muose", (A. S. in my Recollections), **TS**, 1947, No.1, pp. 64-74.
   Also Domas Jasaitis, "Aleksandras Stulginskis", **TS**, 1970, No.
   1(31), pp. 156-177.
2. Cf. K. Čibiras, ed. **Arkivyskupas Jurgis Matulevičius**, Marijam-
   plė, 1933; C. Reklaitis, **Il Servo de Dio Giorgio Matulaitis**,
   Rome, 1955; J. Vaišnora, **Kelias į altoriaus garbę** (Road to the
   Glory of the Altar), Chicago, 1969.
3. Cf. **EL**, Vol. I, pp. 370-371.
4. Cf. Kun. Pranas Manelis, "Vyskupas Justinas Staugaitis", **Suvažiavimo darbai** (Proceedings of the Lithuanian Catholic
   Science Academy), Rome, 1961, pp. 272-274.
5. Cf. **LE**, Vol. XXXII, pp. 462-464.
6. Cf. Vaidevutis-Lapelis, **Prelatas Kazimieras Šaulys**, 1949.
7. Cf. **LE**, Vol. XXXII, p. 462.
8. Cf. **EL**, Vol. I, pp. 372-373.
9. Cf. P. Maldeikis, ed. **Vytautas Endziulaitis**, (Chicago, 1965).
10. Cf. Jan. Tumėnienė, "Antanas Tumėnas", V. Vaitiekūnas, "Va-
    lios principų žmogus" (A Man of Will Power and Principles),
    and Kan. Pr. Penkauskas, "Prof. Antanas Tumėnas tremtyje",
    (Prof. A. T. in Exile); all three essays appeared in **TS**, 1948,
    No. 4, pp. 287-301.
11. Cf. Juozas Eretas, "Prof. Dr. Pranas Dovydaitis", **Suvažiavimo
    darbai** (Proceedings...), Vol. IV. pp. 229-236; **EL**, Vol. II, pp.
    101-103.
12. Cf. Juozas Eretas, "Jo Eksc. Vysk. Mečislovas Reinys" **Suva-
    žiavimo darbai** (Proceedings...), Vol. III, pp. 475-481; **LE**, Vol.
    XXV, pp. 84-86.
13. Cf. Juozas Eretas, **Stasys Šalkauskis** (New York, 1960).
14. Cf. J. Brazaitis, ed. **Didysis jo nuotykis** (His Great Adventure),
    (New York, 1971).

15. Biographical sketches of others can be found in various volumes of **Lietuvių Enciklopedija** and **Encyclopedia Lituanica**.

17. ON THE SIDELINES

1. Dr. V. Viliamas, "Lietuvos seimai...", **TS**, 1957, No. 1 (14), p. 38.
2. Ibid., p. 41.
3. Ibid., p. 42 et seq.
4. Although the actual participants in the several acts of the coup d'etat were army officers, there is little question that the idea was born in the minds of the Nationalist leaders who were also the masterminds and leaders of it. From the very beginning the Nationalists of that time could not get used to the idea of parliamentary democracy and never failed to seek ways and means to "improve" it. At the same time a strong desire for power coupled with minimal popularity among the electorate acted as a constant irritant to the Nationalists. On the other hand the Populist-Socialdemocratic coalition didn't help its own cause by broad sweeping reforms and other policies having a tendency to threaten the stability of the country and antagonize the majority of the populous. (For a balanced essay on the subject cf. Domas Jasaitis, "Gruodžio 17 d., perversmas — The Coup d'Etat of December 17th —, **TS**, 1967, No. 1(28), pp. 15-32. The author makes good use of several memoirs of respected eyewitnesses of the event — high Government officials all — and presents an analytical and objective view of the overthrow of the Populist-Socialdemocratic Government).
5. Some political students of that period fault the Christian Democrats for (a) participating as a party in the coup, (b) electing Antanas Smetona to the Presidency, and (c) taking part in Augustinas Volemaras' Cabinet. Documented facts and accounts of many eyewitnesses do not sustain the first allegation. However, it is true that Christian Democrats in the Diet voted for A. Smetona, and also true that two C. D. leaders briefly participated in the post-coup Cabinet. These two acts were based on documented solemn assurances by A. Smetona and Nationalist leadership that the new Government will abide by the Constitution to the letter. (As a matter of fact President Smetona while taking the oath of office — administered by Archbishop Juozapas Skvireckas — swore to "Almighty God... to safeguard the Constitution and the laws..."). Alas, the oath

and other solemn promises were soon broken by the new President and his Party's leadership.

6. Cf. Dr. V. Viliamas, op. cit., p. 65.
7. Dr. Pakštas labeled it "semi-democracy, semi-dictatorship". (Cf. **Lithuania and World War II**, Chicago, 1947, p. 22).
8 Cf. Leonas Sabaliūnas, "Lithuanian Politics Under Stress: Ideological and Political Development Before the Soviet Occupation" **Lituanus**, 1968, No. 3, pp. 29-42.

18. UNDER THE YOKE OF TYRRANY

1. Cf. Mykolas Krupavičius, "Krikščioniškoji Demokratija..." p. 63.
2. Quoted from Dr. D. Krivickas, **Soviet-German Pact of 1939 and Lithuania** (Hamilton, 1959), p. 13.
3. Ibid., p. 14
4. For a complete text see Prof. Kazys Pakštas, Ph. D., **Lithuania and World War II**, pp. 70-72.
5. Here is what Lenin himself said about seizure of small nations: "Any incorporation of a small and weak nation into a large or strong State without the definite, clear and voluntary desire to that effect of that nation" and especially "if this nation is not accorded the right to decide the problem of the form of its political existence by a free vote — implying the complete withdrawal of the troops of the incorporating or merely strong nation — then the incorporation is an annexation, i. e. an arbitrary appropriation of a foreign country, an act of violence". **Collected Works of Lenin**, Vol. XII, p. 13; cited from E.J. Harrison, **Lithuania's Fight For Freedom**, Chicago, 1952
6. Various aspects of Lithuania's occupation by the Soviet Union are authoritatively analyzed in several books and essays. Among them: Bronis Kaslas, ed. **The USSR-German Aggression Against Lithuania** (New York, 1973), V. Stanley Vardys, ed., **Lithuania Under the Soviets** (New York, 1965), Dr. D. Krivickas essay "Lithuania's Struggle Against Aggression and Subjugation" in **Twenty Years' Struggle for Freedom of Lithuania**, Juozas Audėnas, ed. (New York, 1963), U. S. House of Representatives, Select Committee on Communist Aggression, **Third Interim Report**, Albert N. Tarulis, **Soviet Policy Toward The Baltic States** (Notre Dame, 1949), Prof. Mykolas Romeris, **Lietuvos Sovietizacija** (Sovietization of Lithuania), (Published under pseudonym X Y in Augsburg, Germany, 1949), Dr. Pet-

ras Mačiulis, **Trys ultimatumai** (Three Ultimatums), New York, 1962).

7. Cf. V. Stanley Vardys, op. cit., Chapter 4.

8. Ibid.

9. Cf. Alg. M. Budreckis, **The Lithuanian National Revolt of 1941** (Boston, 1968).

10. Cf. A. Gražiūnas, "Nacinė Lietuvos okupacija" (Nazi Occupation of Lithuania), TS, 1966, No. 1(27), pp. 51-76 and TS, 1967, No. 1(28), pp. 60-86.

11. Cf. J. S-is, "Lietuvių tautos kova prieš SS legioną" (Lithuanian Nation's Fight Against an SS Legion), TS, 1948, No. 2-3, pp. 107-124.

12. Of the memoranda only a copy of the third one is known to exist. The originals of all three documents are presumed to be lost. For the text of the third memorandum (in Lithuanian) and comments cf. M. Krupavičius, "Memorandumai hitlerinės okupacijos Generaliniam Komisarui Kaune" (Memoranda to the Commissioner General of the Hitlerite Occupation in Kaunas), TS, 1959, No. 2-3(18), p. 87 et seq.

13. Ibid.

14. Cf. Stasys Lušys, "The Origin of the Supreme Committee for Liberation of Lithuania" in Juozas Audėnas, ed. **Twenty Years'...** (New York, 1963), pp. 25-39.

15. Authors's translation from original Lithuanian.

16. For an in-depth analysis of legal aspects of the authority and scope of the Supreme Committee (Lith. abbr. VLIK) within the framework of international law and diplomatic precedence cf. Dr. K. Šidlauskas essay "Supreme Committee for Liberation of Lithuania as Representative of Lithuanian National Interests", in **Twenty Years...** (pp. 93-117).

17. See Note 6 above. Also K. Pelėkis, **Genocide** (West Germany, 1949); Supreme Committee, **Appeal to the United Nations on Genocide;** Dr. Domas Jasaitis, **Nacionalsocialistinis ir komunistinis genocidas Lietuvoje** (Nationalsocialist and Communist Genocide in Lithuania), (Rome, 1969); Dr. Kazys Pakštas, "Colonialism and Genocide in Lithuania", **Lituanus**, 1960, No. 3 pp. 96-103; Dr. J. Savasis, **The War Against God in Lithuania,** (New York, 1966); Bishop Vincent Brizgys, **Religious Conditions in Lithuania Under Soviet Russian Occupation** (Chicago, 1968); Vytautas Vaitiekūnas, **A Survey of Developments in Captive Lithuania** in 1963-1964 (also second volume covering the period 1965-1968); Dr. V. Mar., "Krikščionybės likimas

235

кomunizmo režime" (The Fate of Christianity Under Communism's Regime), **TS**, 1959, No. 2-3(18), pp. 1-33; P. Rimtautas, "Sovietinis ateizmas Lietuvoje", (Soviet Atheism in Lithuania), **TS**, 1968, No. 1(29), pp. 60-72 and 1969, No. 1(30), pp. 37-63; **Lithuanian Catholic Church Chronicle** (Both in Lithuanian and English editions; see Bibliography).

18. See 6 and 17 above. Also: Juozas Daumantas, **Partizanai** (The Partisans), (Chicago, 1962); K.V. Tauras, **Guerilla Warfare on the Amber Coast** (New York, 1962); **Lituanus,** 1962, No. 1-2 (a special issue on Lithuanian Resistance).

19. The Department of State Bulletin, July 27, 1940, Vol. III, No. 57, p. 48.

20. Prime Minister Winston Churchill's letter to Foreign Secretary Anthony Eden of January 8, 1942. (Quoted from Winston S. Churchill, **The Second World War, The Grand Alliance,** p. 585).

21. Ibid., p. 584.

22. For Lithuania's international status and related questions of sovereignty, provisions of international law, etc., see works by Dr. D. Krivickas, Dr. V. Stanley Vardys, Dr. Kazys Šidlauskas, and Dr. Bronis Kaslas noted elsewhere, as well as, Dr. Martin Brakas, "Lithuania's International Status — Some Legal Aspects", **Baltic Review,** October 1970, No. 37, pp. 43-59 and August, 1971, No. 38, pp. 8-41; Dr. Stasys Antanas Bačkis, **Katalikų Bažnyčios doktrina apie tautų apsisprendimo teisę** (Catholic Church Doctrine in Regard to National Self-Determination), (Rome, 1961).

23. Although the Nations of the world occupied by their own internal problems, and in many instances seeking selfish goals in international life, from time to time by words of their leaders, if not deeds, remind the conscience of the free world the newest Colonial Empire — the Soviet Union.
    about the gross injustices being perpetrated to this day by

    The Council of Europe on July 29, 1960 adopted a Resolution in which it states in part that "illegal annexation (of Lithuania, Latvia and Estonia) took place without any genuine reference to wishes of the people." (Cf. **The Baltic States and the Soviet Union,** (Stockholm, 1962), p. 9.

    In one of his speeches John F. Kennedy said: "We must never — at the summit, in any treaty declaration, in our words, or even in our minds — recognize Soviet domination of Eastern Europe. We must condemn Soviet abuses, and constantly remind the world that millions of people are enslaved by Soviet rule" (February 4, 1960).

In an address to the General Assembly of the United Nations John F. Kennedy on September 25, 1961 said: "The tide of selfdetermination has not yet reached the Communist empire where a population... lives under governments installed by foreign troops instead of free institutions".

Right Hon. David Ormsby Gore, MP, British Minister of State for Foreign Affairs said also at the United Nations in 1960: "In that same period (since 1939) the whole or part of six countries, with a population of 22 million, have been forcibly incorporated into the Soviet Union; they include the world's three newest colonies: Lithuania, Estonia and Latvia."

Former Secretary of State of the United States John Foster Dulles in a Statement to House of Representatives of the U.S. Baltic Committee on November 30, 1953 said inter alia that "we must be sure that the captive peoples know that they are not forgotten, that we are not reconciled to their fate, and above all, that we are not prepared to seek illusory safety for ourselves by a bargain with their masters which would confirm their captivity."

A.E. de Schryver, former President of N.E.I. (Nouvelles Equipes Internationales) declared: "Christian Democrats of the West don't believe that status quo in East and Middle Europe could at any time satisfy the aspirations of the people of those countries, and therefore those nations must be assured of freedom and the right of free self-determination."

One of the really bright spots as far as Christian Democracy's international responsibilities are concerned is the Resolution passed by the Third World Congress of UIJDC (International Union of Young Christian Democrats). Because of its clear commitment to the freedom of the Baltic countries it is reprinted here in extenso. (See Appendices). 35 nations and nine international organizations participated in the Congress which took place in Montevideo, Uruguay, May 11-18, 1969. Lithuania's delegation was chaired by Dr. Jonas Norkaitis, Stuttgart, W. Germany. (Cf. UIJDC, 3rd World Congress, **Resolutions**, Rome 1969.

237

19. IN POLITICAL EXILE

1. Cf. Juozas Eretas, **Kazys Pakštas** (Rome, 1970.)
2. Cf. **EL**, Vol. III, p. 387. See also Leonardas Šimutis, **Amerikos Lietuvių Taryba** (Lithuanian American Council), (Chicago, 1971). The book has a substantial English language section. and States), (London). A deeply meaningful, incisive, and
3. Cf. Juozas Eretas, **Mažosios tautos ir valstybės** (Small Nations elegantly written eassay on the subject.

20. CHRISTIAN DEMOCRACY CHALLENGED

1. The realization by Christian Democracy that it does have international responsibilities is very vividly demonstrated in a collection of Resolutions and Declarations by various CD international bodies during the period 1947-1973. (Cf. **La Democratie Chretienne Dans le Monde.** Resolutions et declarations des organisations internationales democrates chretiennes de
2. A similar thought was eloquently expressed by Dr. Antonio 1947 a 1973. Rome, 1973).
   Alvarez Restrepo, Colombia's Representative to the United Nations in a speech before that body, when he said: "The problem of freedom is indivisible, and it is an arbitrary action to rise against oppression of one sort and with regard to one system when the total freedom of man has been wiped out in other parts of the world".
3. Cf. Dr. V. Mar., op. cit.,
4. Cf. A. J. Kasulaitis, **Komunizmo grėsmė emigracijos kryžkelėje** (Communism's Threat at the Crossroads of Exile), (Cleveland, 1969).
5. Cf. Francis Cardinal Spellman, "Pax Sovietica", **Cosmopolitan,** November, 1946. For thoughts on Christian peace cf. Pope Pius XII Christmas Radio address of December 24, 1948.
6. "Marxism is materialism. As such it is mercilessly antagonistic towards religion..." Lenin, quoted in **TS**, 1959, No. 2-3(18), p. 4; "Religion is the opium of masses" — Karl Marx; "Every religious idea, every idea about God in an unspeakable ugliness", Lenin's letter to Maxim Gorki, quoted from **TS**, 1959, No. 2-3 (18), p. 6; etc., etc.
7. "Catholic doctrine in regard to State and Society was always based on the principle that by the will of God (all) Nations comprise one Community, having one goal and common re-

sponsibilities˙. (Pope Pius XII, op. cit.) A similar thought is expressed by Bob Goudzwaard: "Politics which is driven by the real love of neighbour described in the Gospel, cannot and may not discriminate between subjects of my own and foreign races..." **(A Christian Political Option, Toronto, 1972, p. 33).**

APPENDICES

1. Translated from original Lithuanian text. (Cf. **TS**, 1968, No. 1(29), pp. 11-17.
2. Translated from orginal Lithuanian text. (Cf. **TS**, 1963, No· 1(23), pp. 1-6.

BIBLIOGRAPHY

The following bibliography embraces primarily a limited list-ing of writings in English, as well as, Lithuanian mostly of political, economic and historic nature. They include both the works of general information and some specific studies on particular subjects. Although an effort has been made to include the most pertinent works in English, Lithuanian material is also included for the benefit of those readers whose command of the Lithuanian language will enable them to pursue the material covered in more detail.

On the other hand since this study on the Lithuanian Christian Democracy is the first comprehensive outline of the subject matter in English, by necessity the great majority of the source material used (such as it was) is in Lithuanian. Even this literature is a small part of source material which at this time is anian Christian Democracy) are scattered among several periodicals published both in English and Lithuanian. A list of some of these unavailable because of Lithuania's occupation.

A number of substantive articles on Lithuania (and on Lithu-periodicals is provided with the hope that they may be helpful to the reader.

Audėnas, Juozas, editor. **Twenty Years' Struggle for Freedom of Lithuania.** New York: ELTA Information Service, 1963.

Bučys, Vysk. P. P. **Atsiminimai,** I ir II dalys. Surašė prof. Z. Ivinskis, redagavo J. Vaišnora, M.I.C. Čikaga: Lietuviškos knygos Klubas, 1966.

Baltic States Investigation. Hearings Before the Select Committee to Investigate the Incorporation of the Baltic States into the U.S.S.R. Washington, 1954.

The Baltic States and the Soviet Union. (Reprinted from a Report of the Council of Europe, with a preface and supplementary comments). Stokholm: Estonian Information Center, 1962.

Brizgys, The Most Rev. Vincent. **Religious Conditions in Lithuania**

Under The Soviet Russian Occupation. Chicago, 1968.

Budreckis, Alg. M. **The Lithuanian National Revolt of 1941. Boston:** Lithuanian Encyclopedia Press, 1968.

Chase, Thomas G. **The Story of Lithuania.** New York: Stratford House, 1946.

Christian Democracy in Central Europe. New York: Christian Democratic Union of Central Europe, 1952.

Daumantas, Juozas. **Partizanai.** Chicago: Į Laisvę Fondas Lietuviškai Kultūrai Ugdyti, 1962.

Encyclopedia Lituanica (In English). Three volumes, from A through M. Boston: Juozas Kapočius, Publisher. Published between 1970 and 1973.

Eretas, Juozas, **Kazys Pakštas: Tautinio šauklio odisėja** (1893-1960). Roma: Lietuvių Katalikų Mokslų Akademija, 1970.

————, **Stasys Šalkauskis (1886-1941).** New York: Ateitininkų Federacija, 1960.

Gerutis, Albertas, ed. **Lithuania 700 Years.** Translated by Alg. Budreckis. New York: Manyland Books, 1969.

Harrison, Ernest J. **Lithuania 1928.** London: Hazell, Watson and Viney, 1928.

————, **Lithuania's Fight For Freedom.** New York: The Lithuanian American Information Center, 2nd ed. 1952.

Jonikas, P. **Lietuvių kalbos istorija.** Chicago, 1952.

Jurgėla, Constantine R. Ph. D. **History of the Lithuanian Nation.** New York: Lithuanian Cultural Institute, 1948.

————, **Tannenberg (Eglija-Grunwald),** 15 July, 1410. New York: Lithuanian Veterans Association "Ramovė", 1961.

Kaslas, Bronis J. ed. **The USSR-German Aggression Against Lithuania.** New York: Robert Speller and Sons, Publishers, Inc., 1973.

Koncius, Dr. Joseph B. **Vytautas the Great Grand Duke of Lithuania.** Miamia, Fla.: The Franklin Press, Inc., 1964.

Krivickas, Dr. D. **Soviet-German Pact of 1939 and Lithuania.** Hamilton: Federation of Lithuanian Canadians Hamilton Branch, 1959.

Lietuvių Enciklopedija. 36 volumes. So. Boston: Lithuanian Encyclopedia Press. Published between 1953 and 1969.

Lietuvos Katalikų Bažnyčios kronika. (A collection of Nos. 1-7 of the Lithuanian Catholic Church Chronicle, a publication of Lithuanian underground.) Chicago: Contributors to the Lithuanian Catholic Religious Aid, 1974. (In Lithuanian). Four of these Chronicles are published also in English in separate booklets by the Lithuanian Catholic Priest's League: No. 4 —

From the Catacombs, No. 5 — Christ Behind Wire, No. 6 — Out of the Depths, No. 7 — Desecrated Shrines.

Living in Freedom. A sketch of Independent Lithuania's Achievements. (A collection of essays by 13 authors on various subjects) Augsburg: Lithuanian Information Service, 1948.

Mačiulis, Dr. Petras. Trys Ultimatumai. New York: Darbininkas, 1962.

Manning, Prof. Clarence. The Forgotten Republics. New York: Philosophical Library, 1952.

Norem, Owen J. D. Timeless Lithuania. Chicago: Amerlith Press, 1943.

Pakštas, Dr. Kazys. Lithuania and World War II. Chicago: Lithuanian Cultural Institute, 1947.

——————, Le Climat de la Lithuanie. Klaipėda: 1926.

——————, The Lithuanian Situation. Chicago: Lithuanian Cultural Institute, 1941.

——————, Baltijos respublikų politinė geografija. Kaunas: 1929.

Pelėkis, K. Genocide: Lithuania's Threefold Tragedy. West Germany: Venta, 1949.

Račkauskas, Konstantinas. Lietuvos konstitucinės teisės klausimais. Autoriaus leidinys. Vermont: 1967.

Romeris, Mykolas. Lietuvos sovietizacija. Augsburgas: Lietuvos Teisininkų Tremtinių Draugija, 1949.

Senn, Alfred Erich. The Emergence of Modern Lithuanian. New York: Columbia University Press, 1959.

——————, The Lithuanian Language. Chicago: Lithuanian Cultural Institute, 1942.

Simutis, Anicetas. The Economic Reconstruction of Lithuania After 1918. New York: Columbia University Press, 1942.

Sruogienė-Daugirdaitė, V. Lietuvos Istorija. Chicago: Terra.

Stanys, Dr. A. Lithuania. Augsburg: Community of Lithuanian DP's in Augsburg, 1946.

Sūduvis, N. E. Vienų vieni. Brooklyn: 1964.

Supreme Lithuanian Committee of Liberation. Appeal to the United Nations on Genocide. Lithuanian Foreign Service.

Šapoka, A.Lietuvos istorija. Fellbach-Wuerttenberg: Patria, 1950.

——————, Vilnius in the Life of Lithuania. Toronto: The Lithuanian Association of Vilnius Region, 1962.

Tarulis, Albert N. Soviet Policy Toward the Baltic States: Estonia, Latvia, Lithuania, 1918-1940. Notre Dame, Indiana: University of Notre Dame Press, 1959.

243

Tauras, K. V. **Guerilla Warfare on the Amber Coast.** New York: Voyages Press, 1962.

Vaičiulaitis, Antanas. **Outline History of Lithuanian Literature.** Chicago: Lithuanian Cultural Institute, 1942.

Vaitiekūnas, Vytautas. **Lithuania.** Second revised edition. New York: Lithuanian National Foundation, 1968.

Vardys, V. Stanley. **Lithuania Under the Soviets: Portrait of a Nation, 1940-1965.** New York; Frederick Praeger, 1965.

GLOSSARY OF PERIODICALS

AIDAI. Lithuanian Cultural Monthly Magazine, published since 1946 first in West Germany and now in the USA by Lithuanian Franciscan Fathers.

ACTA BALTICA. Annual publication of the Institutum Balticum (Koenigstein in Taurus, West Germany).

THE BALTIC REVIEW. Published in New York by the Committees for Free Estonia, Latvia and Lithuania, in 1953-1971.

ELTA. Information Service of the Supreme Committee for Liberation of Lithuania. ELTA Bulletins are published in New York, Paris, Munich, Rome, Sao Paulo and Buenos Aires at various intervals in Lithuanian, English, French, German, Italian, Portugese and Spanish languages, and present information and documentation on current events and problems concerning Lithuania.

JAUNIMO ŽYGIAI. (Deeds of Youth). The magazine for youth for civic education and Christian Democratic politics. Published 1955-1962 in Cleveland, USA, by the Youth Section of the Lithuanian Christian Democratic Union.

JOURNAL OF BALTIC STUDIES. Published since 1970 by the Association for the Advancement of Baltic Studies.

LITUANUS. Lithuanian Quarterly. Published in the USA since 1954 by the Lituanus Foundation.

TĖVYNĖS SARGAS. (The Guardian of Homeland).
1. 1896-1904: Lithuanian Catholic monthly newspaper published by a group of priests in Czarist occupied Lithuania and printed in Tilžė (Tilsit), Lithuania Minor because of prohibition of Lithuanian press by the Russian Government.
2. 1917-1920: weekly newspaper for civics, politics, science, literature and economics. Published in Lithuania by the Lithuanian Christian Democratic Party.
3. 1947-Present: non-periodic magazine for politics and social sciences. Published first in West Germany and from 1950 in the USA by the Lithuanian Christian Democratic Union.

DATE DUE